The Majority Press

FROM KINGSTON TO KENYA

DUDLEY THOMPSON is Jamaica's High Commissioner to several African countries, including Nigeria, Ghana, and Namibia. He currently resides in Lagos, Nigeria. He was educated as a teacher at the Mico Training College in Jamaica. After a short period as headmaster of a rural school, he joined the Royal Air Force during World War II and saw active service as a Flight Lieutenant in the Bomber Command over Europe. In 1946 he was awarded a Rhodes Scholarship and entered Merton College, Oxford University, where he studied Jurisprudence and obtained a Bachelor of Arts and Bachelor of Civil Law. He then qualified as a Barrister-at-Law at Gray's Inn, London.

After his studies, he practiced law in Kenya and Tanganyika and became actively involved in the liberation movements of both countries. He returned to Jamaica in 1957. He was president of the Bar Association for several years and became Queen's Counsel in 1962. He has practiced law in many Caribbean countries and has played an effective role in the independence movements of both Belize and the Bahamas.

Participating in the politics of his own country under the leadership, first of Norman W. Manley, and later, Michael Manley, he spent many years as Senator and Member of Parliament. He also served in turn as Minister of Foreign Affairs, Minister of Mining and Natural Resources, and Minister of National Security. He has represented Jamaica in many international forums, including the United Nations and the Organization of African Unity, and he was Jamaica's chief representative to the Law of the Sea Conferences. He is accredited, among other achievements, with introducing the Ombudsman into Jamaica. He has been awarded the Mico Gold Medal, the Order of Jamaica and the Order of Balboa.

From Kingston to Kenya

The Making of a Pan-Africanist Lawyer

by

Dudley J. Thompson

with Margaret Cezair Thompson

TM PRESS THE MAJORITY PRESS
Dover, Massachusetts

Library of Congress Cataloging-in-Publication Data

Thompson, Dudley.   From Kingston to Kenya: the making of a pan-Africanist lawyer /
by Dudley J. Thompson with Margaret Cezair Thompson.
     p.   cm.
  Includes index.
  ISBN 0-912469-29-3 : $10.95
  1. Thompson, Dudley. 2. Lawyers — Jamaica — Biography.
3. Lawyers — Africa, East — Biography. 4. Jamaicans — Africa, East — Biography. 5. Law — Africa, East — History. 6. Kenyatta, Jomo — Trials, litigation, etc.   I. Thompson, Margaret Cezair. II. Title.
KGT28.5.T47A3 1993
340'.092 — dc20
[B]

                                  92-36237
                                       CIP

First published in 1993.
10 9 8 7 6 5 4 3 2 1
The Majority Press
P.O. Box 538
Dover, Massachusetts 02030

Printed in the United States of America.

Contents

Jamaica, 1961 — referendum on West Indian federation

Foreword

This is a welcome and exciting account of a 20th century version of a diasporic African's odyssey back across the Atlantic and Continental Africa to Kenya, but not before completing the triangular route which has been the cause, occasion and outcome of the historic encounters between Western Europe, Africa and the Americas for half a millennium. Dudley Thompson, the protagonist of this odyssey draws on the authority of the lived reality of himself and all those who, as descendants of slaves, remain fueled by the primal desire for freedom, social justice, ancestral certitude and human dignity. His journey is from his deeply rural village in Jamaica, to 'Mother Britain' where he fought on the side of the Allies against obscenities of fascism and pursued higher learning, ironically as a Rhodes Scholar, then to Kenya as part of the struggle against imperialism and racism, its hand-maiden, and finally back home where as a political activist he helped to realize the dream of fellow-West Indians becoming the creators of their own destiny. The challenge of the tale is worth telling. The richness of the experience is worth the reading.

Professor Rex Nettleford
University of the West Indies

Preface

About midnight on October 20, 1952, Jomo Kenyatta, a leading political figure in Kenya at the time, was abruptly awakened from his sleep at his home in the quiet, peaceful highlands of that country. He woke to look down the bore of six rifles pointed at him and held firmly by African soldiers (askari) surrounding his bed at Githunguru, 20 miles from Nairobi. His room in the small wooden house was filled with armed soldiers and policemen.

The lights were on, and the European officer in charge addressed him in the clipped, impersonal tone reserved by the English military for dealings with "natives" which left no doubt as to who was in charge of the colony.

"Get up Kenyatta. You are to come with me now. You are being detained by order of his Excellency the Governor. Get dressed and come with me immediately."

Jomo Kenyatta sat up, bewildered by this sudden intrusion.

"What is this all about? Who are you and why have you brought guns into my house? Am I being placed under arrest?"

"You may take one suitcase with clothes. You will be taken from here and detained at Her Majesty's pleasure. Hurry. Get moving."

"Where are you taking me? Please send this to my lawyer," and he wrote on the back of an envelope: "DUDLEY THOMPSON, MOSHI, TANGANYIKA. COME TO DEFEND ME. JOMO."

The officer took the envelope and placed it in his large military safari pocket.

"A state of emergency has been declared. The jeeps are waiting outside. We must be off before daybreak."

Passing through Kenyatta's mind, bewildered as he must have been, may have been a conversation which had taken place between us months before.

"Jomo, sooner or later they are going to arrest you."

"With things the way they are, I wouldn't put it past them to try something like that. Anyway, if they do, I'll be depending on you to represent me."

It was happening now.

Getting dressed in the early hours of that morning in his heavy corduroy trousers, leather coat and bright beaded belt (the "kinyatta"), he must have been wondering: "Where am I being taken? Will Dudley hear in time?"

He took his packed suitcase, looked around the room and reached for his sturdy, carved, elephant-hand cane. Outside the jeeps were waiting. There were more askaris, more guns.

Later, Kenyatta recounted being whisked off in the dark early hours to a military aerodrome which he recognized as being just outside Nairobi. Together with several armed guards, they boarded a plane. Flying steadily north, then disembarking in a semi-desert area, he reckoned that they must be either in Ethiopia or near the border. The language being spoken around him was strange; he thought he recognized a northern tongue. After waiting in little more than a zinc-covered shed, seated on a bench with his suitcase, he heard another vehicle approach and stop. Commands were shouted, and to his surprise and temporary relief, five men were hustled into the room. They were none other than his own close friends. All but one were executive members of the political movement, the Kenya African Union (KAU) of which he was president. Suddenly they were all shouting together, "What is happening? Why are we brought here like this?" There was a sense of relief in being among friends but there remained the persistent overhanging fear that they were all about to be victims of some unjust police action. The stories were all the same. Taken from bed they were only told that Sir Evelyn Baring, the recently appointed governor, without previous warning had declared a state of emergency, because of an alleged terrorist campaign by Africans, and especially the Kikuyu, being waged against the Europeans. Further they were somehow assumed to be leaders of this "savage revolt."

That envelope and message were never delivered to me. Subsequent events were to prove that these were the first efforts taken to "eliminate" Kenyatta and the others in order to stifle the nationalist cause.

As soon as I heard the news of his detention on the radio I started to get in touch with the authorities in Kenya. They proved to be most unhelpful and refused to disclose the whereabouts of the detainees. If it were not for the fortuitous presence of a certain European living in Kenya at the time, who happened to be in the isolated court at Kapenguria, Kenyatta would not have been able to get the message through to the outside world, and more especially, to me. I may never have heard about his plight or indeed his location early enough to be of assistance. How that European got a second message through to me in the tiny picturesque village called Moshi, where I was living at the time, a village nestling in the foothills of Mount Kilimanjaro, and what followed from this, forms a large part of this book.

For weeks, long, puzzling, dreary weeks, Kenyatta was locked away in a remote semi-desert corner of Africa, far from civilisation. There was no news. He received only the drifts of occasional rumour from itinerant merchants infrequently passing with their wares on camel back. He heard repeated rumours that the Mau Mau was a native insurrection operating in many parts of Africa and spreading throughout the country. He also heard that it consisted of a secret society of which he was said to be the leader. One of the bits of news that came through to him was that two prominent African chiefs, both of whom he knew, had been killed by the Mau Mau for collaborating with "the enemy," in this case the Government. He also heard shortly after his internment, that the Mau Mau had claimed their first European victim, Eric Bower, chopped to death by *pangas* (sharp machetes) in his home. Until his arrest the allegations against the Mau Mau had been limited to minor crimes such as the mutilation of cattle, theft of guns, harassment of collaborators, terrorising the labour force on European farms etc. Such more recent serious news strengthened his hope that the government and settlers would become aware that their accusations against him were a serious mistake, that they had made a grave miscalculation, and that his detention would not provide some kind of "tidy conclusion" to the crisis. These escalating crimes while he was off the scene should have demonstrated that they were dead wrong. They stubbornly refused to view it in this manner and what ensued was the beginning of a civil war.

This war soon began to spread like a forest fire throughout the country. Eventually it found its way into the court room of Kapenguria in the infamous trial which lasted over several months, and which brought to Kenya a team of illustrious international lawyers. It occupied much prominence at the time in the media, not only in East Africa, but in several European newspapers including *The London Times,* as well as newspapers in Asia. This "war" was waged in the towns and farms of Kenya, and deep in the heart of the Aberdare Forest where Mau Mau warriors maintained a para-military base for the next ten years, right up until his release from prison, and the independence of Kenya.

The trial that took place at Kapenguria was no ordinary trial. Neither were these ordinary times. Kenyatta certainly was an extraordinary person.

This was a period of high crisis in East Africa. A British prime minister announced to the world at large that he discerned "the winds of change sweeping over Africa." A Jamaican lawyer practicing in East Africa at the time, I was caught up by fate in the very eye of the storm.

Just over twenty years after these dramatic events I was leading a delegation from my country, Jamaica, to several countries in East and West Africa. I was at that time Jamaica's foreign minister. I went therefore not only in my official capacity, but as a man who had shared some deep and strong experiences with these developing countries.

I had ventured into East Africa in the first instance as a young and inexperienced lawyer in a gut response to what may be described as a "call of the blood." I had remained there for several years during which period crucial events took place. This was the period which witnessed the birth pains of both Kenya and Tanganyika as independent countries. Although they were neighbouring countries it will be seen that there were several striking contrasts between their political development both in structure and struggle. Notwithstanding, they shared at the same time the same objective — the goal of independence, freedom from colonial rule.

I lived in both countries, and took an active part in their differing approaches to independence. It is as an eyewitness that I shall present the story of the unusual turbulence in the greater part of this book.

On this subsequent visit in 1974, among the places visited by our delegation was the Isle of Goree off the coast of Senegal. This was a most emotional event. Tears fell silently as we looked around the old fort. It was really an old stone warehouse, facing the Atlantic and used for "storing" thousands of Black slaves, men, women and children, on their last stop in Africa before they were shipped to provide labour for the white settlers of the New World. There we saw still embedded in the thick walls bits of rusty chains, manacles and other cruel relics of that infamous trade. The guide said, and I find it easy to believe, that "Every time visitors come to this spot, there are always tears of shame and sorrow."

I tried to imagine what it must have been like for the slaves from different nations, speaking different languages, brought from deep in the heart of Africa, forced to march many miles, often through hostile country, to this prison for mixed human merchandise. Here many saw the ocean for the first time in their lives. Here they were chained to the walls, strangers, unable to communicate with one another, sharing in common only their inhuman degradation. They would be wondering what was happening and what next to expect in these altogether strange circumstances. They must have been driven in collective bewilderment and frustration into a psychological trauma close to insanity. Some lived through this and even through the indescribable Middle Passage across the seas. Some survived to the extent that they succeeded in creating the Caribbean societies of Jamaica, Cuba, Trinidad, Barbados, Haiti, Grenada, Dominica and others. So then, in 1974 at Goree I was contemplating history in flesh and blood terms, the real history of my ancestors. I felt more strongly than ever the likeness between my people in Jamaica and my brethren in Africa.

On that occasion our Senegalese host welcomed us with traditional warm hospitality as "prodigals" returning to the Motherland. Despite his good intentions I felt forced to set the record straight on that point. I replied that we could hardly accept the description of "prodigal," as our ancestors had neither left home willingly, nor had they taken any worldly goods to squander along the way. In fact they had been through Hell itself, and many had fallen by the wayside. I told him that he was looking at the descendants of some of Africa's fittest sons, for only the strongest could have survived the ordeal of man's inhumanity. We West Indians, I added, who carried the blood of Africa in our veins, for our very survival had been forced to accept and adopt Western culture. This brought with it some advantages, and today we are in the position to contribute considerably to the progress of the Motherland.

It is only fair that you should know something about me as author, as it is what I saw and experienced that I am about to share with you.

The first half of my life found me in countries remote indeed from Africa. As a Black colonial I was educated in a country school in Westmoreland, Jamaica and later at the Mico Teachers' Training College in Kingston, Jamaica in the nineteen-thirties. As an officer member of Bomber Command in the Royal Air Force during World War II, I had a ringside view of the destruction of much of Europe. As a Rhodes Scholar at Oxford in the late nineteen-forties, I came to know some of England's brightest and best. I later participated in the great Pan-African Movement and met such legendary characters as Kwame Nkrumah of Ghana, Dr. W. E. B. DuBois of America, George Padmore of Trinidad, and C. L. R. James, illustrious author, philosopher, lecturer, who only recently passed away. As a lawyer I was one of the international team that went to the defence of Jomo Kenyatta, who survived the most farcical political trial of this century to become later the first president of his liberated land.

The book in a sense is about a man thrust into direct confrontation between an Empire and a colonized people in their post-war struggle for political and economic independence.

1 Darliston

I grew up in the village of Darliston, in rural Jamaica. It was a typical country hamlet where we were brought up as loyal subjects under the peace and protection of the British flag. There we cultivated sugar cane, also bananas, oranges, pimento, ginger and other spices, coffee, cocoa, tobacco and other crops which were shipped off to enrich largely absentee English landlords and other members of the plantocracy. These for their part discharged a paternal obligation of suzerainty by enforcing law and order in the colonies while they lived a life of luxury at home.

This is not to suggest that I suffered under a feeling of exploitation or inferior political status at the time. I was born in the system. I grew up happily in almost bucolic surroundings, where the land was fertile, the countryside lush, fruitful and healthy and where political problems never disturbed our thoughts. I was just one of millions of contented country boys.

My brother Carl and myself were very happy in Darliston. He was two years older than I in a family of eight. The last four of us were born not in Jamaica but in Panama but have never considered ourselves anything but Jamaicans. Both my parents were among those Jamaicans who in those days from time to time migrated abroad in successive waves to Cuba, to develop their sugar, to Panama, to help build the Canal, to Costa Rica, to lay down the railway, and to the United States in search of employment at the beginning of the century and "to better themselves." My father had gone over to Panama as a teacher to work for the Americans who had contracted a contingent of West Indian labour for the construction of the Canal. My very earliest years saw me growing up in settlements like Colon or Silver City. My playmates were the children of Barbadian, Trinidadian,

Jamaican and other West Indian neighbours. This environment made the novelty of the fresh Jamaican countryside ever so much more enjoyable, when I came there.

It was 1927 and I was about eleven years old when our mother told two of us that she was sending us there. "Dudley, you and Carl must get yourselves ready. You are lucky, for you are the first ones to go and join your father in Jamaica. We others will join you later on, if the Good Lord spares us." In childlike faith, we accepted this just as a bit of good news, for although we had never been there, it had always been accepted in a feeling of joyful expectation that the entire family would one day return to this fabulous land. To me, it was a picture drawn from tales at my mother's knee, as a land where oranges, bananas, papayas, mangoes and other fruit grew on trees just outside your own door, and where you got milk from a cow that you actually owned.

My father had gone ahead to resume his profession as a teacher in the parish of his birth, Westmoreland, in the western part of Jamaica. We did not have the money to return all at once, so he had gone to prepare for our phased return. My mother worked at home as a seamstress and raised the large family. We had so far grown up in a Panamanian town where we had only seen apples, pears, plums, oranges and other imported fruits neatly displayed on fruit stands, and much as I longed to taste them they were well beyond our slender means. I had never been within yards of a cow, much less seen one being milked. I was therefore glad to receive this news, and heartened by the consolation from my mother that she "would soon come over with the rest of the family as soon as we saved enough money to do so."

Carl and myself travelled on a rough and uncomfortable passage called "steerage." This meant that we lived and slept on the deck of a ship. Passports were not required in those days, but some "papers" were handed by my mother to a "stout" lady returning to Jamaica, who promised to keep an eye on us during the voyage. Although we had never been at sea before, the hardships of the voyage meant nothing to us in the blissful innocence of childhood and we actually enjoyed the new adventure and our first experience away from home. After about four days at sea we were overjoyed to see land at last. My first view of the island was that of a large rock, beautifully covered with palms and other foliage.

The ship was tied up at a pier and there was much bustle and no formality as we disembarked. A young lady came forward and claimed us. She had been sent from the country by my father. We had few belongings, and I was very disappointed that she whisked us off from the pier, by a taxi, directly to the railway station. Thus started a long but scenic journey, passing over mountain, river and dale, through dark tunnels, past cascades rushing down the hillsides and over bridges, for a little over a hundred slow miles, which is almost the length of the island.

"Why didn't you take us to see Kingston?" I asked.

"Your father is awaiting you at home in Westmoreland. We can't stop as the train only runs once a day."

Her accent had an attractive lilt, quite different from that to which we were accustomed. I was very sorry not to be able to see Kingston which, from the tales I had heard, was almost the "capital of the world." The new railway experience, however, compensated for the disappointment. I spent most of the time at the window in the aisle outside the small cubicle where four people sat facing each other.

"What is that?" I kept shouting and pointing out new sights from time to time. This time it was a woman astride a donkey, with a large hamper basket on either side, riding probably to market.

"Come here Carl! Quick! Look at the boy leading a whole flock of goats."

These, like the small waterfalls, ferns and other sights were my first scenes of this enchanting countryside. I knew right away that I was going to enjoy my new exciting life here.

Filled as I was with excitement, one of the high points of my joy, amounting to sheer ecstasy, was when I tasted my first Jamaican meat patty. To begin with I was hungry, not having eaten since we left the ship. The patty vendor was a large, smiling, amiable woman who passed from coach to coach on the moving train. She carried what looked like a small stove but which was really a homemade, tin, warming pan with a lighted taper in a bottom compartment. She was very buxom and wore a large apron and a plaid bandana head wrap.

"Hot meat patty! Fresh meat patty! Buy yu patty!" she sang in a loud falsetto, over and over again as she passed from one car to the next.

This is a particular type of meat pie in which highly spiced meat is enclosed in a delicious crumbly crust. It is served hot and is as appetizing to smell as it is satisfying to taste. Carl and I bought several, to the delight of all the onlookers. The vendor was pleased as she exclaimed (partly in disbelief) to herself, "See here! Is really the first time these two young gentlemen ever see patty! Is where they come from?" and she went on, pleased with the sale: "Hot patty! Fresh patty! Buy yu patty!"

Eventually, exciting as it was, as the day went on, we grew tired. I was glad when our caretaker Miss Clarke said, "All right boys, this is where we get off." The train wheezed to a stop at a quaint little country station called Montpelier, which we were informed was the nearest stop to home. "Is it far from here? How do we get there?"

"No, It's not far. See that little van over there? The red one? That is the Royal Main that always meets the train. It goes near to where we are going." She pointed to a small van with a large "R.M." ("Royal Mail") painted on its side.

We all piled in, some carrying baskets in their laps. The driver hardly seemed to notice the discomfort of his passengers and proceeded at a dangerous speed along the winding mountain road to Darliston. I had never seen such a precipitous road nor such a confident driver before. I prayed. After several stops to let off passengers, which relieved my breathing considerably, we finally disembarked at Darliston. This was little more than a village square with a petrol pump, a shop, a shoemaker's house and a post office shed. It was a short walk from here, and the only way to reach home. I felt greatly relieved to depart from that van, tired as I was.

After walking for about half an hour along an unpaved road we entered a gate which led us for a few yards between what must have been a school-garden on the left and a playground on the right to a small school building at the top of a slight rising. Here we had our first view of the teacher's cottage which was to be home, our final destination. It didn't look promising. In fact, it was a downright disappointment. I had not been expecting anything grand. The truth is, I hadn't given it a thought, but this bungalow, surrounded as it was on two sides by a thick cluster of banana trees, signified neglect. It was not my idea of home, even after a long and tedious journey. I uttered another silent prayer, this time that my mother would soon come on the scene and do whatever was necessary to restore a semblance of the comfort that up to now I had been used to.

The next few days found us trying to adjust to the new surroundings. The people we met were very kind and respectful to "teacher's" two young boys. It was nice to see so much vegetation growing around. There was so much to learn from an outdoor life. Carl kept pointing out the differences.

"The roads here are so bad. Maybe that is why they use so many horses and mules and donkeys."

"Yes. I haven't see a car for days. And do you notice that most of the children go barefooted except on Sundays when they dress up to go to church?"

As the glitter of novelty began to wear off I began to ask myself, "Why did my parents want to leave the convenient modernities of city life to come out to this 'charming' backwardness 'to live'?" This puzzled me for some time. The truth, which I could not know at the time, was that our parents believed that we should grow up where we had our own roots, where we would be owners and not tenants, and in which surroundings we would eventually appreciate a full sense of our own dignity. Our status as a colony did not interfere with this natural desire. At that time the question of independence had not yet come to dominate the political agenda. In fact, we often felt proud to be British citizens, and to share the same flag, the Union Jack, as part of the mighty British Empire.

In Jamaica my father would never earn half as much as he earned in Panama, but there, and more particularly in the Canal Zone, which for all intents and purposes was administered by the U.S.A. as part of their territory, there was the ubiquitous and unmistakable presence of a colour bar. The racial distinction and the lack of equality between Black and white people that went with it was everywhere. They were officially described as gold and silver employees, the Black (or silver) being in all cases the inferior class. They were constantly reminded of their "proper place." There were gold schools for white children, silver for Black, separate gold and silver post offices, restaurants, hotels, cinemas, and even in death, the gold and silver cemeteries assured that there would be no fraternisation in the after life. Black people only visited the gold (white) residential area if they were working there, as maids, caretakers, gardeners or garbage men. In Jamaica there had never been such obvious signs of discrimination based on race. My father had never felt himself a second class citizen in his own land. He regarded racial discrimination as odious and did not want his children growing up in an atmosphere where this was accepted. While enjoying the facilities, if not the fleshpots of Panama, my parents longed for the freedom "at home," in Darliston, Jamaica. Even here far into rural Jamaica, where the people were poor, without electricity, running water or indoor toilets, and with little education they preferred to stay where they could enjoy the overriding feeling of ownership and equality, a sense of dignity that even their colonial status had not denied them. It was that great American, Paul Robeson, on a visit to Jamaica, who exclaimed to the press of the world, even before independence, "This is really the first country in which as a Black man, I've felt truly free."

Both the school and the cottage were owned by the Church. The Church played a great part in the history of education in the country. Our house was on eight acres of land, which was considered in local terms as of considerable size. Most peasant landholders had to sub-divide this among descendants. The majority of peasants worked for someone else as a labourer for day wages. Many were landless squatters on the estates and lived just above subsistence level, but their expenses were minimal. Living standards were low. The land was fertile, the people lived in happy community spirit. The climate was healthy and perpetual summer made it easy to live. You do not miss shoes if you are not used to wearing them. We had no electricity and used two kerosene lamps in the house. We kept one on the dining table and carried the other around as required. The house had no running water, but we were more fortunate than most as just outside we had a large stone tank set squarely in an excavation. Water was collected from the roof which served as a catchment. This was led into the tank by a simple gutter made from tin. We drew the water as desired by a bucket tied to rope which we let down into the tank. Most people in the countryside of rural Jamaica who have no tanks walk in some cases considerable distances to fetch water daily from spring or stream. We soon got used to the familiar figure of children balancing kerosene tins of water on their heads as their daily chore before and after school. We had an outdoor pit toilet, and also an outdoor kitchen, as separate wood-built structures. The kitchen had an open fireplace and a wood-burning stove. This was used for cooking or roasting for the table, as well as for the animals. Food supply was ample, and in that part of the kitchen we stored potatoes, bottles of honey, and other food crops. We grew almost everything the family needed and had enough for sale to the local higgler who resold it at the markets. We also raised animals — pigs, goats, chickens and a few cows which I soon learnt to milk. In season we had mangoes, grapefruit, pineapple, oranges, star apples, guavas and other fruits. Most farmers raised these crops as well as tobacco, peas, tomatoes, carrots, yams, spices — such as ginger and pimento — and other vegetables. Aside from these we reared a few donkeys to carry loads, and mules and horses which we learnt to ride. I quickly learnt to love the country life, waking with the cock's crow at the farmer's dawn, to draw water from the tank by bucket and feed and care for the animals.

I learned to ride horses and climb trees. I learned to distinguish the sounds of birds, the leaves of trees, the seasons when fruits like guinep, mangoes, or star apples ripened. It was a new world unto itself. News travelled only by mouth, and very little news of the outside world penetrated to disturb the peaceful surroundings.

In those days, the school teacher, as an educated man, was one of the most respected pillars of rustic society. When I speak of my father as one such educated man, I mean it in the old colonial sense. Teacher Training Colleges had been established for those Black people who showed the greatest promise at the elementary school level. They were originally trained to go out into the countryside and teach the sons of ex-slaves. They taught a few basic subjects such as reading, writing and arithmetic, and since the schools were largely supported by the churches to instil religious instruction, they also taught their pupils to sing hymns, memorise passages from the Bible and go to church.

Such teachers would casually come across Shakespeare, Dickens and perhaps, Rudyard Kipling. It was considered sufficient to know who these writers were, and to absorb somewhere along the line that Shakespeare was the best, but that they were all good, for they were all British and therefore, the best in the world.

To the people of Darliston my father was a veritable oracle. They would come to him with all their problems which, in a society about sixty-five per cent illiterate, were often simple difficulties like reading a letter, or drafting a reply for same. He acted as village arbiter and minor disputes were brought to him. He advised generally and was the sole subscriber in the district to the daily newspaper, which came by post a day or two late, and which was our only connection with Kingston and the outside world.

The teacher was respected as the local leader in all civic matters, and his lifestyle set the standards of conduct emulated by all around. He had, as a matter of custom, to attend all weddings in the area, and make what were to them learned speeches (largely because they understood very little of what he said since it was in "proper" English and, therefore, "superior" to their tongue). It was considered a mark of some disfavour if he were absent from a funeral. No public ceremony began until Teacher Thompson and his family arrived.

His own father, my grandfather, Constantine Thompson, had also enjoyed a distinguished reputation in that part of Westmoreland. He was the Black overseer on a large estate owned by a wealthy white landowner, Mr. T. R. Williams. My grandfather's wife, Eliza, the child of slaves, was born on that estate. Eliza bore him eleven children, but she looked after many more as Constantine sent her a steady flow of chiefly young girls, workers on his estate who were pregnant by him. "Mooma," he would say, "You are queen of the house. I rule the property." He is reputed to have sired 117 offspring. But he was a good provider, and looked after all of them. There is still a town called Thompson Town in Jamaica. One of the many stories about this man is that because he was the patriarch or head of the clan, almost everybody there was distinguished by their Christian name. Reputedly the biggest and certainly the most important Black man around, as overseer on the estate, he continued to be in charge of all the workers after the abolition of slavery. Although literate, he was otherwise completely uneducated, and probably never went to school. He knew cattle, was good at his job, and Mr. Williams had confidence in him, recognised his leadership qualities, and was fond of him. He was a lay magistrate, that is a local justice of the peace and tried minor cases, or differences such as domestic disputes from the village. I learnt about him from my elders and some of his offspring (my relatives) who spoke of him with pride. It is said that when he made his periodic visits home at Christmas, Easter or Summer (he spent most of his time on the estate, away from home) he travelled — all 280 pounds of him — with an entourage, on a mule. En route, which took several days, there was much drinking, feasting, and at some villages he would settle grievances, administer mild floggings or other punishment and ride on, preceded by the outriders who went ahead to announce and prepare for his arrival. Although my father never enjoyed this aura of esteem, he was awarded great respect for his education, and later, because he had actually travelled abroad and seen the outside world, this respect grew. This, few people in Darliston could ever hope to accomplish.

My mother added her own contribution to my father's prestige. She was light-skinned, almost white in complexion, had long brown hair, and was attractive in a a healthy outdoor kind of way. In those days only the light-skinned Jamaicans were able to obtain the higher levels of employment, in hotels, stores, etc. They always received preference. My father's prestige was consequently enhanced by having her for a wife, and the more so as the union produced children of a "richer" colour. Before marriage she belonged to a fairly wealthy family, the Steeres from Christiana, an inland town where her father, a Jew, owned a small inn, the Savoy Hotel. On her mother's side she was the great-great grand daughter of a General Crawford, the Scottish Commanding Officer of the British Army in Jamaica. Very proud of this ancestry, she would often display to us as well as to visitors, pieces of silverware, explaining "See the 'C' stamped on it. That stands for Crawford, my great-great grandfather." He was buried at Porus in Jamaica and his tomb can be seen at Lang Syne Presbyterian Church. A proud and hard-working woman, she always seemed to be cooking in the kitchen, sewing in the living room, or getting dressed up to go to church. I think I received a special share of her love because I was the last son, and was always reading, or lolling on the floor near to her as she sewed on a machine and spoke to me always about Jamaica. I overheard her boastfully saying to a neighbour, "Dudley is going to go far. He reads all the time." She certainly spurred my ambition. I would run home from school just to show her that I had got all my sums or spelling right. Then even a maternal kiss or pat on the head, not to mention a penny for a cake, would make me feel ten feet tall and on top of the world.

Though our cottage was not much larger than those of small farmers in the district, we appeared in many ways to be better off. For one thing, we wore shoes. Many people, and almost all the children, went barefooted, except on Sundays, when they went to church. We had Sunday shoes as well as everyday ones. I remember my father making the suggestion which, of course, we readily followed, that we need only wear socks on Sundays or special occasions. Another distinction was that we kept house servants, a cook, gardener and general help, all of whom formed part of the household. Usually they were poorer relatives who welcomed the better food and more comfortable lifestyle, growing up with us and helping to look after the farm animals and to perform the thousand and one things to be done in the field.

Mother, who was a seamstress, was fortunate, unlike other women, and could do her work indoors. Most of the neighbours' wives and daughters, to earn money, did work outdoors with the men, like weeding the gardens, reaping crops, picking coffee or rinding oranges, that is, rubbing the fruit over a funnel like instrument with short spikes and extracting the oil which flowed through a funnel below to be collected and sold. I always felt it was such a waste, as the oranges were picked before they were ripe, and thrown away after the extraction. Others like Miss Annie, a neighbour who lived across the wall, were road-builders. She broke stones for five days each week and was paid a pitiably small sum by the road superintendent for really arduous labour. I watched her daily as she took up her seat on a large stone in the open under a frail shed, a mere covering of branches from the coconut palm providing shade from the fierce rays of the sun. Her head was wrapped in a brilliant bandana headkerchief which was covered with a broad rimmed straw hat. She smoked a small clay pipe and talked to herself as she worked, that is, when she wasn't calling to the toddlers around to bring up more stones to be broken with the small hammer she used with monotonous dexterity. The children ran about, playing on the property, while she sat and worked by the roadside, keeping an eye on them, and reducing the rock to just smaller than fist-size. She would continue to work, tending a small pot on the fire made up between three stones for a stove. I watched her with interest and silent sympathy. At the end of the week, the superintendent would come around on horseback on his route of inspection, exchange a few words with her and "measure" the stones. He would then pay her the miserable sum of about five shillings (about a dollar). She did this back-breaking work, as her mother had done before her from early dawn to sunset. I made a silent resolution that when I became a man, I would stop this degrading practice. Somehow Miss Annie, like some of the other women, found time to bake at home. She made coconut cakes, fruit preserves, and corn pone, which she sold from door to door along the road to the market on Saturdays, market days. She carried these goods on a large tray, balanced expertly on her head as she walked, puffing her pipe for many miles. The farmers' wives who took much larger loads like yams, tins of sugar, or other farm produce, would convey them by donkey, with two hampers one on each side. They walked together and gossiped loudly along the road. It was their "day out" and they looked forward to it as breaking the monotony of an otherwise dull week. They all wore large aprons with outsized pockets over their dresses. Coins jingled in those pockets. Sometimes they tied the money in a handkerchief and stuck it in their bosom. I wondered how it didn't fall out.

With this hard-earned money and the crops they grew, people did not starve in the countryside. But there was another kind of starvation, a kind that haunted me daily, and gave me ever-increasing bitterness. Here there was no public entertainment, no social activity, or even a public library. I was intellectually isolated. There was no facility whatever to lift one from that small community where everyone knew everyone else and nothing changed from day to day. The nearest I came to relief was attending church on Sundays, three miles away, to which we all rode on horseback. My father's school room was sometimes used on those days for what was erroneously described as a "pleasant Sunday afternoon." Here Teacher, acting as Master of Ceremonies, would produce "on stage," after much coaching, the best singers and reciters in an interminable programme in which almost every eager volunteer "got a chance," and the "pleasant afternoon" would drag into "weary night." Now and then an itinerant officer from the Ministry of Education in Kingston would come to the village, bringing a movie projector in his van. For days before, this welcome event would be advertised by word of mouth and the entire district would turn out to enjoy it. For many it would be the first time they would see a movie. A borrowed sheet would be hung up before the shop in the square to form a screen. Benches would be brought from the school by eager volunteers. For about an hour before the showing began, these benches would be occupied beyond comfort by jostling children who pushed and scuffled noisily to secure a seat. While the projector, now removed from the van, was being set up by the driver, the older, more inquisitive children would follow his every movement. They helped to erect speakers, attached power lines to the dry battery of the van which was the source of power, and helped generally in the preparation of the showing. Eventually while all were seated and even more were standing around, we would sit for about two hours, watching the acting of Lillian Gish, John Gilbert, Pola Negri or some other famous Hollywood idol of the period, not missing a single word or gesture, and marvelling at that world where everyone was white, and rich and handsome.

Another rarity was the radio. We owned one which was operated by a dry battery, as there was no electricity in the area. Every fortnight or so this had to be sent to town to be re-charged. Whenever this radio was in operation there would inevitably be a small gathering outside our cottage, where the village listened with wonder to the foreign voices broadcasting news from the B.B.C. in far away London, and were amazed at this modern miracle.

At home I read every book I could lay my hands on. These consisted of the old text books, or gifts sent to the school, or others discarded by visitors. I read the *Decline and Fall of the Roman Empire* at least three times. From text books I learnt the mysteries of algebra, before it was taught to me formally at school. Eventually I found myself straining at the leash. Having run out of reading material, I seriously contemplated ways of getting to Kingston. I was really hoping to find a way to escape. It is to be remembered that here at this time my only consolation was the daily newspaper. This I read down to the last advertisement. It was at this time that I first began to notice the name, Norman Washington Manley. He appeared as a defending counsel in the celebrated "Alexander" murder trial which got full publicity in the daily news. Like most young Jamaicans of the day, I was proud of this brilliant Jamaican lawyer, and he quickly became my personal hero. He had fought in the War, had been a Rhodes Scholar, and was now a Queen's Counsel in Kingston.

The realisation that my father could not afford to send me to Kingston for further learning was a source of great frustration to me. My mother, by then together with the family in Jamaica, noticed my impatience and once said, "Don't worry son. It's not your position on the ladder that counts. It's the direction in which you are going that matters." I had become increasingly aware of my position in Jamaican society. In the mornings I would stand out by the roadside holding a goat on a rope so that he could nibble at the tender, fresh, dew-drenched Spanish Needle grass, a favourite food. In my other hand would be a book which I was studying. Now and then a car would pass by with the white family or friends of the estate owners. It would drive past so quickly that I would get just a glimpse of the plantocracy, the neatly dressed children, accompanied by their uniformed Black nannies, in front with the Black chauffeur, their parents comfortably behind. I began to feel a resentment against something I couldn't quite define. It had to do with fairness and the difference in status based on race. Here was I, holding the goat's rope and studying, trying hard to escape from my position tied to a goat. There "they" were comfortable in that motor car, and they could go anywhere they wanted. Furthermore, and even more hurtful, they hadn't even noticed that their car had dusted the goat herd. My mother's wise words mollified me, but they also strengthened my determination to get to Kingston, where the schools were. It was clear to me that only education could solve my problem.

By the age of sixteen I was almost ready to run away from home and get to the city, up to then still unknown to me. Then fate intervened. I was reading a book as usual, high up in a breadfruit tree when my father came below and called to me to descend. His voice was unusually kind and strange. Up to this point I had been a lonely child and there was very little demonstration of personal affection between us. I know he loved me in his own way, but he was always busy. For my part, I was always polite and respectful to my father and obedient to his orders. I felt a little strange, seeing the smile on his face as I came down and recognised his effort to please me. "Dudley," he said, and I could see his gold teeth as his smile grew. He was holding the newspaper. "I have good news for you. You can't realise how great this is. I have just read the results of your Pupil Teacher's Exam, and you have come second out of all Jamaica. This means you are an Exhibitioner and have won a scholarship to college. You do not know how proud I am. Well done Dudley. Your mother will be thrilled to hear." He hugged me for the first time that I could remember. This was the happiest day of my life. I walked on a cloud and immediately began to dream of my future.

This was an examination which was taken by the brightest pupils in the top class in the elementary schools throughout Jamaica and included former students, all of whom took special preparatory lessons privately for this annual examination. It was a qualifying step to further study, but only the first four (exhibitioners) of the hundreds who attempted it were awarded free scholarships to college. I chose to go to the Mico Teachers' Training College in Kingston, where if I passed all my exams the scholarship would entitle me to three years of study and I would be qualified as a school teacher.

2 The Mico

The Mico was the poor man's university. It was founded in 1836 shortly after the emancipation of slaves by some benevolent English philanthropists. In 1670 an Englishwoman, Lady Mico, bequeathed one thousand pounds to her nephew, on condition that he marry one of his cousins. Fortunately, he declined to do so and the money, at her request, was invested by the Mico Trustees for "the purpose of freeing Christian seamen captured and held for ransom by the Barbary pirates of the North African coast." By the nineteenth century, the money having greatly increased and the Barbary pirates being no longer a menace, abolitionists applied for this fund to be used for the education of ex-slaves. Thus the Mico College Trust was founded.

A new phase of my life began in 1934 when I went to Kingston to enter the Mico. I took a letter from my father to a teacher called Mr. Salmon, who lived in Kingston, asking him to put me up for a few days while I took the entrance examination. Mrs. Salmon, the teacher's wife, was very kind and patient with "the boy from the country," and took me into her home at 129 King Street, a middle-class residential area, where I shared a room with her son, a young man older than myself. This was not new as I had been used to sharing a bed with my brother.

I was finally in the great capital. To me Kingston was a very huge place. It really gave me a thrill to walk around the residential area, see new sights and hear the new sounds of the city people. Walking along King Street in those days, one would hear the pleasant sound of people playing pianos inside their homes. In downtown Kingston were the public buildings, such as the court houses, Kingston's general Post office, the larger stores, the famous Myrtle Bank Hotel which was a popular landmark of the city, and the large imposing banks. I noticed that they were all staffed by white-skinned people, English and Jamaican. Some of these stores had large verandahs or roof-top cafes, where oversized, brightly coloured umbrellas over the tables provided shade from the sun. Black people had little stalls or push carts. They travelled along the road shouting their variety of wares. These included sweets, hair-combs, hats, baskets and small table-mats made from straw. I went down to the waterfront where I saw the vendors pressing their craft on new tourists just landing.

Most striking were the tall, Black policemen. They wore a starched khaki uniform, and pith helmets. Colonial regulations prevented them from advancement to officer rank. The resident army was all white from England, though a small battalion of local Blacks was maintained as a relic of the old West India Regiment. This small token group constituted the West India Regiment Band. Their colourful Zouave uniform is still in use today. Said to have been designed in Queen Victoria's day, it presented a great attraction wherever they went. They wore a plaid turban in maroon and cream. A short black and gold embroidered waistcoat over a cream shirt with long, flowing sleeves was gathered at the waist by a scarlet cummerbund which ended in a sash hanging down the right side of their dark blue trousers. Short white leggings, buttoned at the side, covered the tops of regimental boots, polished to a mirror-like finish. This band played on public holidays, at government functions and at places like the Botanical Gardens or parks, and always drew an admiring crowd. The novelties of Kingston, after my sojourn in the country impressed me greatly, even the normal amenities of electric lights, cinemas, and running water and the ordinary water-closet made life much easier, and I made certain that I would not return to the hard life from failure at the Mico.

Although I had won the Scholarship, I still had to sit with the other candidates in the highly competitive entrance examination. This lasted a full week. That year saw 252 young Black men from the country, all natives, sitting in competition. The best fourteen would be selected.

After the exams, we all sat waiting nervously in the hall to be called up for an interview, one by one from the short-list read out by the English principal, Mr. Newman. We were placed in alphabetical order, so my name, if it were there, would be one of the last ones. By then everyone was looking sheepishly around, making meaningless conversation and guesses as to who would not be selected. Finally, to my great relief, I heard my name. I rose and followed Mr. Newman into another room. He spoke in a high falsetto. He had served as a Captain of Infantry in World War I and kept his clipped, military-type moustache. "Young Thompson," he started, "you are two years below the minimum age for acceptance." My heart sank. "However, you have done so well in the entrance exam that the Board has decided to give you a chance. But let me tell you at the outset the rules of this college. Failure in any single subject means that you will be sent back home." His piercing blue eyes bore down on mine, but I thought I recognised a twinkle underneath his apparent ferocity. I never had a better incentive to do well. I recognised my good fortune. The first occasion on which I went into the college library, I was completely overwhelmed. Never before had I ever seen so many books in one room. I was determined not to return to the country without getting my education.

I spent three very happy years at the Mico College and made some great friends there, many of whom still remain close to me. Among them my favourite was Aston Taylor, a remarkable scholar and one of the shyest persons I have ever met. He was elegant, graceful, and always considerate of others. Later in life he qualified and obtained several advanced degrees in Agricultural Science.

He became very restive after some years, as he felt he was not being fully utilised. On one of my visits to Jamaica, he confided in me, "Dudley, can't you get me a different job out in Africa? I'm wasting my time out here. The department sends me all over the countryside, to tell the farmers how to plant yam and potatoes and they all know this better than I. Can you help?" I promised my friend, without having any specific idea, except that I had the ear of some influential people over there. Further, it had always been my dream to attract to Africa as many qualified and interested West Indians as I could to replace the European expatriates that occupied the senior posts in the Colonial Service. I felt as I do now that to us it was more than a job. We have a vested interest in its success. We have a debt to repay that continent.

I wrote to a friend that I had known during my time at Oxford, one Meddi Abbas, who at the time was directing the great Gezira Cotton Project in the Sudan. I got another friend, George Padmore, to recommend Aston and he was appointed. Aston was delighted. Here was a real challenge to his undoubted ability. The Sudanese authorities thought very highly of him, and after years of service there another Jamaican left a good mark on the motherland. He found a canvas sufficiently large to extend himself, and travelled thousands of miles, from the Atlantic to the Nile.

Unfortunately, he died at a very early age after returning to Jamaica, but not before bequeathing to his Alma Mater, the Mico, his invaluable collection of African memorabilia which today forms the nucleus of the Mico Museum.

It was at the Mico, under the tutelage of such greats as the late J. J. Mills, that the idea of nationhood began to take a vague shape in my mind. The social barriers of race prejudice showed themselves much more sharply in Kingston than they had in rural Jamaica. White Englishmen held most of the senior posts and often did not equal the ability of Black Jamaicans placed under them. In fact, the Colonial system provided a convenient dumping ground for many second rate officials who were not quite suitable for the home service. There were, of course, exceptions to the rule. At the time, I, like most Jamaicans, accepted this situation as normal, that the best jobs were reserved for Englishmen. Our resentment to this was, at the most, muted and not widespread. Colonial compliance was the order of the day.

At the Mico I had a very good scholastic record, and played both soccer and tennis. After my three years there, as I entered the formative years of manhood, I began to look forward to returning to teach in the country. I had experienced city-life and came to the conclusion that I preferred to live among country folk. I recalled my early days in Westmoreland and was eager to return to feed the minds of those children who were as provincial and hungry for facts about the world as I had been. As a child I had read my father's magazines, especially *The Crisis,* a Black magazine published by the famous American scholar, W. E. B. DuBois. It published articles on prominent Black Americans who had succeeded in various fields. In its pages I first became acquainted with names like Booker T. Washington, Dr. Carver, Madam Walker and others. People like these, later to be joined by others like Paul Robeson, Norman Manley, J. A. G. Smith, Joe Louis and Claude McKay, became my early heroes. It was with this background, all that I had been exposed to in Kingston and at the Mico, and the burgeoning ideas about my country and my race, that I set out to teach in the countryside. It was 1937, and I was not quite twenty years old.

I placed an advertisement in the daily newspaper, describing myself as a graduate of the college and applying for a post as a teacher. I received a response from a minister of religion some forty miles away in the neighbouring parish. I rode my pedal bicycle some thirty odd miles of bad gravelled stone road, over hill and dale, pushing it some of the time and arrived quite tired and dusty. On my arrival, the reverend gentleman was sitting on his verandah upstairs and spoke to me from his chair. He was past middle age, and pale skinned. Many of his kind were direct descendants of English settlers, or second sons doing a spell in the colonial overseas missionary service. I was still breathing hard from the journey and had dismounted from the cycle at the gate when he addressed me without a word of welcome. "Are you the young man that applied for the post as school teacher at Lacovia?"

"Yes Sir. My name is Thompson and. . . ."

"What is your religion?" he asked.

I explained that I was Roman Catholic, but that I had attended Methodist, Anglican, Moravian and other Christian churches in my time. Further, I had no particular preference as to which denomination I supported.

"Do you play the organ?" he continued.

"No, I do not," I regretted, and was about to add that I was willing to learn when he closed the garden gate interview with, "Well I'm sorry. I need someone who can play the organ at church on Sundays."

I once more mounted my tired bicycle and began the long, lonely journey home in a spirit of dejection that grew mile after mile on the uneven road. I had as company only the painful thoughts of my first rejection as I rode home into the night.

In the ninetenth century a missionary living in Jamaica wrote that he looked forward to the day when "The sable emancipated infants we are now receiving into our schools shall respectfully and successfully occupy their stations in the pulpit, on the bench and at the bar." He was a great deal more far-sighted that many a churchman in Jamaica in the nineteen-thirties who still saw the Black school teacher as a kind of parson's assistant.

It was not long after this that I got my first job as schoolmaster in Albion Mountain, in the parish of St. Mary, the deep rural heartland of Jamaica. The teacher's cottage was a small unfinished house, with basic amenities, but this was compensated for by the people in the district who were very kind and helpful to the "young teacher," as they called me. They brought melons and mangoes and kept my larder supplied with more eggs, Irish potatoes and naseberries than I could possibly eat alone.

On my first morning at school I got up very early, before dawn. I felt quite nervous and alone in the dark schoolroom and I prayed that I would be fit to receive those little children, some of them coming for their first lesson away from home. I wanted to write on their minds the story of their own people. I took down the pictures of British kings and queens and past governors and replaced them with those of Marcus Garvey, Norman Manley (a newspaper print), Booker T. Washington and others whom I felt would be a greater source of inspiration to my own Jamaican people.

I was teaching and learning at the same time, still very much aware that my own view was so limited and colonial. I longed to know, and to be able to teach my students, what was happening to Black people in other parts of the world. In those days there were no text-books that gave any realistic picture of Africa or the Caribbean. The history books taught us only so much colonial history that we would know from acquaintance with Sir

Francis Drake, the battle against the Spanish Armada, etc. No one was learning about Paul Bogle or other Jamaican heroes, and educated people did not talk about Marcus Garvey. Marcus Garvey had been deported from the United States in 1929 and had come back to Jamaica, his place of birth. In Jamaica he was generally thought of as a troublemaker, but his speeches in the nineteen-thirties left a mark on the minds of the Black and uneducated poor. More than anything else, he opened their eyes to the fact that as Black people, they were a force, a factor to be taken into account, not shadows falling behind other human beings but human beings themselves. I had the rather unique experience of knowing Marcus Garvey, from a somewhat peculiar and unfair angle. For years my father attempted to sue him in a court of law for rent he owed.

It had begun in Panama when Garvey was touring that country and "rented" my father's schoolroom for some of his meetings. He apparently never paid my father and for years I heard my father rail against him "This man, who does he thing he is? Fooling a lot of Black people . . . selling pictures of Black Jesus and investing them with titles making them Black dukes and duchesses. Only the King can do that." He had a bad view of Garvey and as a child I absorbed that view: "Garvey was wrong and my father was right." But I stole away a few times to hear him speak. He was a great speaker, but like my father, I couldn't understand how he could sell pictures of Black angels and Black saints. Everybody "knew" that angels were white. It was years later that Mrs. Garvey explained to me that what Garvey was telling people by the very strangeness of those pictures, was that the human qualities, goodness, mercy, self-sacrifice, were not exclusively the features of any one race. Not only Jamaica, but the West Indies, Africa and the entire world of Black people are indebted to this man. He was a genuine Pan-Africanist and to date the greatest mass-mobilizer of Black people in history. His Universal Negro Improvement Association (UNIA) is still alive in many countries. He has been a source of inspiration to many subsequent leaders, including Kwame Nkrumah, N. W. Manley, Bustamante, Nelson Mandela, and others, all of whom have paid public tribute to him as a source of their own inspiration.

At twenty-one I became headmaster of a school at Enfield. It was a much larger school than the one in Westmoreland where I had grown up. It was very near to the estate of R. F. Williams, whose father had been master of the estate when my grandfather had worked there as an overseer. This R. F. Williams, who was in a sense my benefactor — contributing gifts and money to the school — also happened to be the son of the first director of education in Jamaica. The school was also not far from the Frome Sugar Estate where a labour revolt broke out in 1938. This was a demonstration for more pay by the badly underpaid sugar cane labourers.

The news of the unrest leaked out early by "bush telegraph" into the peaceful hills of Westmoreland. The workers on the cane fields were demonstrating for more pay and better living conditions. This revolt soon spread throughout the island. Some of the overseers on the estates were attacked. The police killed some of the workers in an attempt to stop the unrest. In Kingston there was a strike of waterfront workers. The strikers marched throughout the streets, forcing shops to close and overturning cars. Many were arrested before order was restored.

This was when I first began to hear about Bustamente, the self-appointed representative of the workers, who was the man leading the strikes. He had started some months before by writing letters to the newspaper, advocating better conditions for labourers. He later formed a trade union — the Bustamante Industrial Trade Union, or BITU as it was called. People adored him and would obey him without question. Physically, he struck an impressive picture. A tall white Jamaican, standing well over six feet with hair that looked like a lion's mane, he spoke to the people in patois, their own language. It was his language too, for he was not a well-educated or sophisticated man by any means, a genuine pattern of the people's hero.

When Bustamante — or "Busta" as he was popularly called — was arrested, his cousin, Norman Manley, Q.C., took up his cause. The two men were related by virtue of having the same grandmother. Just before Bustamante's arrest, Manley had formed the People's National Party (PNP) with Busta as an early member. With Busta in jail, the PNP held meetings all over the country and helped to keep the trade union alive. The whole country was joining forces against the old colonial line. People were calling for an end to Crown Colony government and for the beginning of representative government based on universal adult suffrage. In 1939 Manley came to Westmoreland on one of his many all-island tours. I went, along with my father, to see him at the market square in Darliston. As a youth I didn't understand everything that he said, but never doubted his sincerity. I'm sure that on that evening a spark flew from the inspired intellect of that great man, and entered the hungry shadows of my mind. It has remained there ever since. He was not fiery like Bustamante, but eloquent — and sincere patriotism shone through every word. Until that time I had been fired with ambition to learn for learning's sake. Now I began to sense a conflict, a battle ahead of me. Manley's words drew a very clear picture for me of an enemy — the foreign oppressor — and a new purpose came into my life. Perhaps it was there, in the market square of Darliston that I began to prepare myself for confrontation. But it would take a great deal more learning and experience than I had at the time. It would take years as a soldier and then as a student in England before I would be able to take part in any actionist struggle or cause.

For the time being I was happy to teach, but I paid attention to the changes suddenly occurring in the country. While Bustamante was in prison, great suspicion and distrust grew up between himself and his cousin. The authorities are said to have told Busta — "Look, your cousin Manley is taking over the country and turning it communist." Manley was, in fact, a Fabian socialist, never a communist, and some twelve years later, purged the party of prominent members suspected of being communists. When Bustamante was released in 1942, he started his own political party, the Jamaica Labour Party (JLP).

Norman Manley, an Oxford man, did not have Busta's vibrancy or warmth. He was a statesman, not a populist, a "brown" man, not a Black; and his party was composed primarily of the petty bourgeoisie. Manley was essentially an outstanding intellectual. He had a programme and plans which took into primary account a profound respect for the democratic process and the necessity to educate his people. For these reasons I greatly admired him and felt that I would join his party — as I did. And I have so remained ever since.

On the other hand, Busta also attracted me. He was a great opportunist, a bread and butter politician, but he loved people. He liked me very much and in later years would ask me to join forces with him. But I am jumping ahead; I will write, later, of my friendship with both these men and my initiation into Jamaican politics.

3 World War II

In 1939 World War II broke out and occupied the front pages of the world's news for the next few years. This sudden and serious outburst of universal proportions naturally relegated to the back burner matters of local significance such as the nascent movement for self-government in the colonies. News of the repeated success of Hitler's *blitzkreig,* his lightning advance and the precipitous retreat of the countries of Western Europe reached us as the first phase of the war was savagely fought out. With England at war, her colonies were at war. In our small way, Jamaica assisted. We appealed for funds, sent comfort parcels to the troops, and one enterprising Jamaican, a Mr. Gordon, opened a Spitfire Fund in the newspaper, where all were asked to donate funds to purchase these fighter planes as a gesture of our patriotism and support. It was a success that got much publicity. Gordon's Spitfire Fund was copied elsewhere in the Empire.

Being a small island and, therefore, dependent on many things, including food and all manufactured goods imported form abroad, we were particularly affected by the submarine campaign of the Germans in the Atlantic. Defence regulations were enacted and we adopted austerity measures. We also launched a successful food production campaign.

A few men managed to slip away silently at their own expense to volunteer for the fighting services. This was especially frequent whenever the newspapers relayed news of the bombing of civilians in places like London and Coventry. At first, the colonies were not allowed to participate in the fighting. In Trinidad there were street demonstrations and rioting because of the hesitation on the part of Britain to let Black men enlist in numbers to fight the war. We would hear about the bombings and we were bursting at the seams with patriotism to go and rescue the mother country. This zeal was a direct expression of colonial submission and indoctrination.

After a while they began to let a few colonials into the army, but there were many restrictions on the ways in which Black people could serve, not to mention how difficult, how nearly impossible it was for them to move up in rank. The colonial office and the governors of the islands had pressured the British Army to take West Indians in, but there were directives from the War Ministry to put every hindrance in the way of advancement. They would not be made officers. Many recruiting officers bluntly refused Black West Indians. Dr. Leo Marsh, later a prominent Jamaican dentist, was turned down by the RAF on the grounds that "he was not of pure European descent." He still persisted in applying, and he went on to become a major in the British army.

One day while I was sitting in a dentist's office in Kingston, to pass the time I picked up a book that was lying on the table. It happened to be Hitler's *Mein Kampf.* I didn't read the whole thing, but came across a passage in which he made the most denigrating remarks about Jews and "Negroes." I decided then and there to join up. I was angry and stung into activity.

R. F. Williams of Enfield, Westmoreland, had been recruiting volunteers. When I went to him and told him that I wanted to go, he was very encouraging. Two of his sons had enlisted while at school in England. One, unfortunately, lost his life in action. The other became a nurse and, coincidentally, looked after me when I was later wounded in the Royal Air Force (RAF).

I felt that a new adventure was ahead of me as I went for my various tests and medical check-ups in Jamaica, preparatory to going abroad for enlistment. One doctor in Jamaica asked me: "Why are you going over there to get your head shot off? What does it mean to you whether it's Germany or England who wins?" I was appalled. How could a patriotic Jamaican say a thing like that?

I said, "Take my pressure and sign me up!" He had been abroad as a student in Edinburgh and his eyes had already been opened to truths about imperialism. Mine had not.

My family were very much against my going. They felt I had a great future as a teacher, and that I might one day even become a school inspector. Like the doctor, they were certain I was going abroad to be killed in a war that had nothing to do with me.

As a young man going to enlist in a war in a strange country, there was a certain romantic satisfaction in the adventure. We went over to Britain on one of the banana producers' boats. Among the recruits were Roy "Ashes" Ashman, a first-class pianist who later, unfortunately, died in the Air Force, David Chance, and "Bully" Edwards — an ex-policeman, who was lost in action over the sea. R. F. Williams was one of the directors of the banana producers, and he came over on the ship with us. I remember the ship stopped in Canada and we were told that we could get off there, enlist and train for a year. But we all declined the offer. We wanted to get across the Atlantic and have a chance to fight before the war was finished. At this time I was completely single-minded about the adventure. I was going to become a pilot and I was going to be up in the air fighting a dog-fight with a German and I was going to shoot him down and come back home. This would give me the satisfaction of proof against Hitler's racism. These were the fantasies of a young colonial.

We reached England as civilians and split up to join the various divisions of the army, air force, etc. England was a great new country to me, unlike anything I had imagined. For the first time, I saw poor white people, the English working class — uneducated, unclean, sweeping the streets and carrying coal. In the colonies white people are the governors and the social elite. They are people who are clearly "better off." That was the first shock. The next was the war itself. Though we arrived during a black-out, it wasn't until I went to buy an ice cream and got an unsweetened, watered-down version of the real thing that it dawned on me: I thought, "How on earth can they make ice cream without sugar? This country must really be at war."

It was incredible seeing Buckingham Palace. All colonial people hear this name in awe. To actually see the place where the King lived was, for someone from the colonies, second only to seeing heaven itself. And then, in turn, we seemed strange to the English. People would come up to us and touch our skins and our hair — not meaning to be disrespectful. Many just hadn't seen Black people before.

Volunteering for the RAF had its difficulties. One of the questions on the form which I had to fill out was "Are you of pure European descent?" I answered "yes." When the recruiting officer queried me — thinking I hadn't understood the question — I challenged him to prove otherwise by a blood test. I think he gave up in disgust or frustration. This overt racism existed even under the stress of war, in the early stages.

Life as a volunteer airman proved to be a thrilling adventure. There was first the experience of immediate transformation from the casual ease of civilian life to the robot life of army discipline. At one moment it seemed I was sitting, talking man-to-man with a fellow, and next he was shouting

Royal Air Force, June 1945. Dudley Thompson second from left

me to attention: "Don't you know to stand when you are speaking to an officer?" Now, for the first time as an adult, I took orders, obeyed them, and actually came to enjoy the fact that I was no more than a cipher, an insignificant part of a great machine that possessed on its own, a collective glory. Although you were a mere "cog" it allowed you or practically forced you to share in a comforting friendship and camaraderie with fellow "sufferers." Under the insatiable scrutiny and drive of drill inspectors (a breed apart), I not only learned to polish boots to dazzling perfection and brass buttons to a glittering gold, but to take pride in the uniform, develop an *esprit de corps* and hold in healthy respect those who were in a superior position. We were all, in a sense, back at school, and being in a strange country added to the excitement.

There were early hardships — like sleeping on the floor of the air raid shelters in the tree-lined streets of St. John's Wood, London. But the morale was very high. We sang as we marched through the streets of London, songs that the men had composed in the shelters and in the barracks. There were some great humorists among us: "If we'd thought we'd have to march, we'd never have joined the blooming infantry. . . ." (Chorus) "You shouldn't have joined, lad, you shouldn't have joined." They became increasingly ribald as time went by. We sang loudly and lustily as we marched.

Dudley Thompson, July 27, 1946

After a few weeks of ITW — Initial Training Wing — we were separated and sent to different stations. There were many stages and at each stage aptitude tests and examinations which determined whether you would actually go on to more difficult and advanced training. I learned elementary ground lessons, "foot slogging" as we called it, meteorology, mathematics, principles of flight, and so on. By this time, the RAF had relaxed its rules on the recruiting and promoting of Black men, but I knew that if it came down to a choice between me and an Englishman, I would be promoted only if I had done far better than he had. In short, I had to win by a knock-out. I was determined to fly, and kept being transferred from station to station for more training. On posting one took all one's earthly possessions, including spare uniform and personal effects, in a cylindrical kit canvas bag that seemed to weigh a ton. We hoisted this on our shoulders everywhere. At the new station we made new friends, and with luck, sometimes kept a few of the old ones.

I passed the tests that determined I would be air crew and was sent to elementary flight training school, but still had to get more training and do more tests to determine whether I would be navigator, pilot, wireless operator, bomb aimer, gunner, etc. Here, I learned things like the Morse Code, and aircraft recognition, where we used flash cards to identify at a glance the type of aircraft, friend or foe, principles of flight astral navigation, etc. At last, I was taken aloft with an instructor, and it is hard to describe the joy of being up there, for the first time, entering a whole new dimension. It was strange at first, recognizing houses by the shapes of their roofs, and people like small dots, seeing only the tops of their heads. Also, reading a map from the air is a wholly different procedure and somewhat difficult at first. After a certain number of hours of instruction, and generally getting used to being in the air, the instructor one day said, "Take her up." I remember walking proudly past all the other cadets. "Going solo today," I proudly announced, for this was the day we were all looking forward to. "Watch me." I stuck out my chest and carried my bulky parachute pack over one arm just as I used to carry my saddle to horse as a country boy in Westmoreland years earlier. This time there was a plane, an empty plane waiting for me to try my skill.

To be up there alone, watching the instruments, knowing you cannot lose control of them or you lose the plane (or worse), is one of the most exciting experiences. Further, landing the place was not just a matter of putting down the plane, you had to land her the RAF way, that is, lightly on three points. The front and two rear wheels should touch down simultaneously. Otherwise there would be a bump, hop and skip operation. It was to be a matter of precision-flying all the way. The instructors were demanding but very good, all experienced pilots, many on temporary rest from active service in operational battles of war with a squadron.

After this first day of flying solo, I got much satisfaction and increased confidence in cross country flying. With the world at your feet, imbued with new thoughts, you have a strange feeling of power. At this stage getting used to each other — the plane and myself being fused as into one unit — I learned much about the English countryside. I loved to look at the change in terrain over the seasons. From above I saw snow coming down on the naked trees. Autumn was my favourite season, presenting me with coloured forests of yellow, brown, gold and green leaves, Nature's carpet laid in the forests for us to admire.

Actually I experienced my very first snowfall while I was posted to Scotland (a thoughtless act, posting heat-seeking West Indians to what we thought must be the coldest part of the world). You could always tell the men from the tropics because we walked around in many ridiculous layers of clothes and blankets to keep ourselves warm. But I loved seeing the snow, especially that first time. I awoke and looked outside to see what appeared to be a different country. The snowflakes like millions of tiny white feathers were floating silently down to cover the earth.

It was only about three months before I was promoted to the rank of Leading Air Craftman (LAC). I was well liked by my tutors, and did well in all my tests. The things I did poorly were exercises such as marching, polishing my belt, boots and military webbing. These were known as "bull . . . ," and I often received censure for my lack of proficiency in these operations. I recall our inspecting officer, on many a tour of inspection in our quarters, shaking his head in despair. We were supposed to be standing stiffly to attention looking ahead, beside our beds where we had laid out our neatly folded sheets and blankets, with shoes highly polished, comb and brush in exact position, etc. There was "old Joe" (he had a remarkable resemblance to Joseph Stalin — hence the nickname), after looking at my less than neat military precision, shaking his head, "LAC Thompson!"

"Sir."

"You are a natural born civilian. Look at that blanket!" The sargeant in charge was less understanding. The result was punishment, serving seven days in the post office, sorting mail. This was a frequent occurrence. In fact I made fast friends with another "miscreant," an English friend, "permanently banished on postal duty." He taught me all the tricks of the trade. There is nothing a soldier enjoys more than receiving mail from home, and we used this to our greatest advantage. It was in the mail room too that I learned from LAC Flint how to play chess. He later became my rear gunner in action.

After doing a certain amount of night flying — that was one of the hardest tests, being up in the air in the dark and having to find your way back home — and also, cross country flying, I was recommended to Cranwell College for officer training. Cranwell is the British version of West Point, a massively imposing place. Matters of administrative authority and Air Force history were taught. It was altogether a very rigorous and comprehensive course of training. As a member of aircrew you were taught a little of everyone else's job, so that in an emergency you could substitute for a lost crew member. Cranwell was not the end of training, however. Now that I had learned to fly, I had to learn how to fight, and was sent to an operational training unit.

On operations, things took on a different atmosphere. Squadron life brought you into direct contact with your reason for being here, namely, war. For one thing, we carried live ammunition on the planes. By this time there was the constant fear of invasion because the Germans had marched across France. It was in Lincolnshire, in a single-engined aircraft, that I had my first accident. I was up there alone and it was an incredibly foggy night. I simply could not find my way or see anything. Knowing Lincolnshire is all lowlands, I took a chance and came down, to see where I was, but I crashed into some trees. Apparently a farmer who lived nearby saw the whole thing and luckily came by with some others and pulled me out of the plane unconscious. Only a few minutes later, the plane caught fire. I only suffered a mild concussion.

After the single-engined aircraft, I moved to "twins" like Oxfords, Blenheims, the Boa Constrictor and the Mosquito. Oxfords and Blenheims were plodders with limited speed and altitude; the Boa Constrictor had much greater firepower. It had cannons which shook the entire aircraft when fired and proved very effective against enemy shipping. The Mosquito was a very fast two-engined aircraft made mostly of plywood. It was used for photographic reconnaissance and often flew out on special missions without any armaments. The toughest workhorse of them all was the Wellington bomber. It was of geodetic construction and could withstand quite a lot of punishment before limping faithfully back to base, often full of holes.

There was a close and friendly feeling in the squadron. Life was a lark. We kept ourselves fit. We flew, sang, drank, danced in the nearest town, shared jokes and truly cared for one another. We exchanged talk of what happened "out there," and generally kept ourselves and each other alert and ready for anything.

The ground crews were marvellous. These were the airforce men who kept the planes in good condition. They knew how much responsibility rested on them, knew we could not get out and "fix it" once we were up there, and would not let us go out with bullet holes in "their" planes. Several times I had to explain how I had managed to get "their planes" shot up. Altogether the ground crew were the most admirable and efficient bunch.

Eventually, I was posted to a Lancaster station. Lancasters were the four-engine bombers which took a heavy bomb load and, in my opinion, were the most effective bombers of World War II. After some flying in these, I was sent to a Pathfinder Squadron and took part in the Pathfinder operations.

Pathfinders were the elite of Bomber Command. They were the ones who went right into the target, investigated and gave specific instructions for bombing during bombing operations. The novel, *A Man Called Intrepid* by William Stephenson, gives an accurate description of these operations. I have great memories of that war period, not all of them happy. We sometimes missed a friend who never returned, like "Ashes" Ashman who flew into a mountain in the fog, and Bully Edwards, the ex-policeman from Allman Town in Kingston who was shot down, it was believed, at sea. His sister, Linda Gardener, who lived in London, was the first Issa Scholar from Jamaica. Linda was always glad to see Jamaican airmen and to cook home-food for us when we were on leave.

The Americans had still not entered the war, and we were flying over Germany and going even as far as Poland. We were suffering many losses; many planes were shot down. (I was wounded in the leg, flying over Nuremburg). But somehow, we never thought or spoke about death, though death was around us. Other people died, but you never thought that you would. For me, the most striking remembrance of raw courage was that of the average working-class man and woman — the civilians in the bombed cities. Every morning they came up out of the underground stations with their bedding and pillows, always with a joke on their lips. They took the war in their stride and never once seemed to consider losing. Churchill's inspiration did marvels for all of us over there, civilians and military alike. We admired his courage.

On the lighter side, I recall the period when everyone was being prepared for invasion by the Germans, who had blitzed their way across Europe and stood poised on the other side of the Channel. There was general mobilization in England. The Home Guard saw old men and women in training. Fire wardens were on the roofs at night with steel helmets and sand buckets ready to put out incendiaries. Metal railings were removed from the fronts of fashionable houses and melted down for cannons. Farmers and their sons, together with veterans of World War I, trained with pikes and sharpened staves to fend off the enemy whom they expected to land any day. England was badly unprepared for war.

At that time I was doing a spell training new air crews for bomber command. Aside from the small smoke bombs which we had for training purposes, we also took on board, at this time, for emergency purposes, a large hundred-pound bomb. We took it up on each flight every day. The men got quite attached to it and treated "Bertha," as they called it, like a pet, scribbling messages all over her smooth casing.

After a while, and especially after the Battle of Britain, the RAF Fighter Command gained supremacy in the air. Throughout Britain, and especially on the coastline, tensions eased considerably. The allies took the offensive with large-scale saturation bombing, and the relief gradually spread. The commanding officer decided we should celebrate, and this was to take the form of a practice bombing run with "Bertha" somewhere in the Atlantic. Our target was a small lonely rock in the ocean, probably a bird sanctuary. The crew was specially selected, as everyone wanted to fly. We chose our best navigator, best bomb aimer, etc., and flew fairly ten thousand feet up where we had a clear run in good visibility. The navigator and pilot were "dead on" when the bomb aimer crept down into the nose of the aircraft and set up his sights — a very complicated procedure. Everyone was waiting for the words: "Bomb fused, bomb doors open," small corrections left and right, then finally, "Bombs gone!"

We were low enough for everyone to see as the pilot banked the plane — that is, he dropped one wing and circled tightly allowing us to look out. We held our breaths and saw the bomb go down, hit, rebound, and fall off without exploding. After a moment's hush and consternation, we broke out into uproarious laughter. The bomb was a dud! We had been flying for weeks with a dud for defence. But, as one of the crew in wry humour suggested: "It could've hit one of the enemy on his head."

I look back on these war years in England as a period of great friendship and warmth. I was treated fairly throughout my training by those in command, and warmly by the Englishmen in ranks, including those under me. Often, they invited West Indian soldiers to meet their families. You know if they said — "I've told my Mum about you" — that the family knew in advance that you were Black. We airmen had more time off than other soldiers, and I spent a good deal of my time off in London where it was always a pleasure to meet other West Indian soldiers on leave. There were people like the late Errol Barrow, who would become Prime Minister of

Barbados and a popular and leading statesman in the West Indies, and the much decorated Ulric Cross from Trinidad, later Trinidad and Tobago's High Commissioner in London. News from home was priceless and the West India Committee, at that time under Lady Davson, was a tremendous help in keeping us up-to-date with home events. One of the favourite places to go was the Caribbean Club in Piccadilly. It was run by a West Indian named Rudy Evans who had been an actor, wrestler and restauranteur in turn, and during the war ran this lively nightclub. West Indian soldiers were famous in England for their dancing. Along with the soldiers were the many West Indian munition workers who worked in the factories, and West Indian students.

At this time too — when I would go to London, and sometimes to Manchester, on leave — I met a number of West Indian and African scholars and intellectuals. Among them were George Padmore, the father of the Pan-African Movement, a mentor to me, and to many who would become world leaders — Ho Chi Minh, Kwame Nkrumah, Jomo Kenyatta. We would often meet at the Caribbean Club or in restaurants and discuss politics. In Manchester, T. R. Makonnen, a die-hard Pan-Africanist, owned a restaurant. He was forever providing West Indians and Africans with free meals, giving them jobs in the restaurant, and providing a place for meetings. One lasting effect on me of this war period was that by 1945, I was coming into contact for the first time with West Indian, African, and Black American soldiers, and with students, writers and blue-collar workers from the British colonies — all of us meeting in the Mother country, the seat of the Empire. Being in England, fighting and suffering with her during the war, had truly opened the eyes of the colonials. Having lain side by side with the English in the trenches and shelters, we felt we had more than proved our equality and had earned the chance for self-government.

That was what the Fifth Pan-African Congress demanded in 1945. It challenged England to honour the principles of the Atlantic Charter signed by Churchill and Roosevelt in 1941 (and later discounted by Churchill, who said it did not apply to the colonies), affirming the "right of all people to choose the form of government under which they may live."

I will speak later about the Congress, held in Manchester, England, towards the end of the war, also about my friendships with Pan-Africanists such as Padmore and Makonnen.

In Manchester I met and married Pearle Cezair who was, at the time, training to become a nurse. Her father, Dr. Hubert Cezair, was a prominent Trinidadian doctor living in Manchester, and her mother, who was Scottish, worked with the Red Cross and often brought home soldiers from the

Caribbean and the United States to meet the rest of the family and to enjoy some home cooking. Everyone in England, the English themselves and West Indians who had been living there, did their utmost to make us feel at home.

Shortly after V-E (Victory in Europe) Day, I was sent from the squadron to be briefed at the Air Ministry in London. I was asked to return home — still in the Service — to advise the government of Jamaica on demobilization of the returning ex-servicemen. I was allowed to take one other RAF airman with me, and I chose my friend Vin Bunting, a pilot officer who was eager to go back to Jamaica. I also travelled with my new wife, Pearle. This was her introduction to Jamaica and to my family.

I had left Jamaica a child, so to speak; now I saw things from an entirely different perspective. My eyes had been opened to the Englishman at home and his brother in the Colonies. In Jamaica, friendships between "them" and "us" were thinner; the English man was always alone and on a higher plane than the Jamaican below him, and yet I had believed — growing up in Jamaica — that racism was not practised by the British; racism was in America, undisguisedly a part of their national policy — but not in Jamaica. There were white schools and Black schools in America; but in Jamaica there were only expensive schools which could only be afforded by whites and a few token Blacks. Hotels and restaurants had the same hard, dividing, albeit invisible, line. We had accepted this blindly and taken pride in the fact that we were British, even if we were poor and could not afford the education, health, and other social benefits that were "in law open to all."

Seeing poor white Englishmen carrying coal on their backs totally destroyed the myth of the white superman of the colonies. The class system, both at home and in England, revealed itself dramatically before my eyes, and it had taken considerable mental adjustment, while in England, to understand the strictures of social relationships which I had not paid full attention to before. Wartime in England was a great university to the uninitiated colonial.

In Jamaica, while working for the Colonial Government as a sort of liaison officer for returning ex-servicement, an incident occurred which really forced me to see the difference in attitude between the English in the colonies and at home. One day, my assistant, Vin Bunting, complained that he was refused sale of some towels from the military stores at Up-Park Camp in Kingston. He had been told that those goods (at much reduced prices) were exclusively for the English soldiers stationed there. I went back in anger to Up-Park Camp with him, to the very same counter where the sergeant respectfully repeated to the officer — myself — the "regulation." I asked to see the written order and was shown an unsigned document to that effect. I then asked to see the officer in charge of the stores, who was also below my rank, for an explanation of what appeared to be sheer racial prejudice. He came in, rather flustered, and denied that there was any prejudice intended, but that there was a distinction between the King's Commission in Britain and in the colonies, a distinction which seemed extremely spurious and unacceptable to me. I solved the matter by pointing out that such distinctions did not apply to us, since we had both been commissioned by His Majesty in England, and, I added forcefully, UNDER FIRE. We had no more difficulty in shopping there after this and the "regulation" was changed.

At this time I was naturally thinking about what I would do in terms of a profession. The RAF had made a very lucrative offer to me for extended service, and I was tempted by it. There would not have been much more to do than I had already been doing, except with much less danger. But I felt that I would find myself at middle age with a comfortable retired life and I would be paid for nothing more than wearing the uniform. I could not think of anything less satisfying to me than being a British officer during peace time at home. It seemed really a useless life and it did not attract me. I planned to go back to England and study. I thought perhaps that I would like to be a medical doctor. Then an incident occurred that put me somewhat in the limelight and gave me an idea of what it would be like to practise law.

One evening at home I received a telegram. It said something like this: "Mutiny on board *S.S. Bergensfiord,* troopship returning airmen. Longitude X Latitude Y. Awaiting Instruction."

The message had been delivered to me because I was the second top ranking RAF officer on the island. My immediate superior was on leave in England. Apparently some disorder had broken out on the troop ship the *S.S. Bergensfiord* and had reached dangerous proportions. In fact, by the time the wire reached me, over a hundred Jamaican ex-servicemen had taken over command of the ship. It turned out, on investigation, that some white Trinidadians had remarked in conversation with some Black Jamaicans, that the Jamaicans had always behaved badly in England, causing the many racial incidents there, and had "let down the side." It was, at best, a tactless remark, and a fight broke out with the Trinidadians retreating in the direction of the first-class cabins, and the Jamaicans following in hot pursuit. When the ship's crew intervened, the Jamaicans brought up willing reinforcements. Mutiny broke out and the Jamaicans took over the ship. The passengers, who included Squadron Leader Webster, my superior, who was returning home with his family, were more or less confined to their cabins for safety.

I immediately alerted the governor by telephone. He was Hugh Foot, later Sir Hugh Foot, and later still Lord Caradon, a minister in the 1966 British government. He was a fine man from a very liberal and enlightened family and became one of the most popular governors of Jamaica. He got my message while attending a formal dinner in Kingston and asked me to inform the officer in charge of the British military detachment at Up-Park Camp, appraise the situation with him, then meet as early as possible at his residence, King's House.

Arriving at King's House, he greeted me in complete evening attire, black tie and all, and said, "Well Dudley, what are we going to do? It's nowhere in my book of instructions." I felt equally ignorant as did the officer who joined us with several aides, and after sitting around a table and discussing it at length, we realised we could not make plans without more information. It was decided that I should go out to sea, board the vessel and report back to them.

A pilot boat took me out to this rendezvous on the high seas. It took some dexterity to climb up the rope ladder onto the ship, but even greater skill to overcome the all-too-eager hands of my comrades-at-arms who were overjoyed to see their old Jamaican liaison officer. Everyone was talking at once, each complaining vehemently about the treatment they had received. It was as if they were suddenly giving vent to years of suppressed discontent. After restoring order, I went to the captain. He was Norwegian and proved very amiable, lucid and informative. He had been expecting me and had been in continuous touch with Kingston. The *HMS Warspite* which had been in the area had been diverted to oversee the disturbance and was hovering nearby. In fact, it had circled the stationary *Bergensfiord* which had been brought to anchor, and the *Warspite* had been using fog horns to order the men to lay down their arms. The Captain agreed that this was only making the situation worse. The Jamaicans had replied to this warning with shouted obscenities. After returning to the men and hearing their story, I communicated with the Governor, who ordered the *Warspite* to withdraw to the horizon while I spoke further with the men. I told them that we had been given word that the docking would proceed in an orderly fashion, that the men's families would be awaiting them and no reprisal or charges brought against them.

Approaching the island, however, the vessel, acting on instructions unknown to me, sailed not into Kingston Harbour where their families awaited them but into a berth at the coaling station in Port Royal. When the men realised what was happening, a tremendous tumult began. They refused to disembark and began to hurl bits of coal, potatoes and other missiles towards the soldiers on the dock, in such a shower that the soldiers ashore took cover behind the cranes and railway cars nearby. Once more, I managed to restore order and they disembarked. But they felt betrayed and expressed it in no uncertain language.

One of the last men to disembark, Corporal Alexander, on reaching the top of the gangplank, turned to deliver a parting shot, a left hook with his fist to the jaw of the British officer nearby. The officer fell and the man was immediately arrested for striking a superior officer. Some days later I got a note asking me to defend Alexander at a court martial at Up-Park Camp. The trial was covered by the local newspapers, in particular, a publication called *Trade Winds* run by Ken Hill, which published the whole case in detail and wrote editorials. It came out during the trial that Alexander and the officer had gotten into a scuffle after Alexander had refused to step-down the gang plank. His refusal was a form of protest, as far as he was concerned. The English had broken their word. I had no experience at this time with matters of law, but managed to argue effectively in his defence and got him acquitted. I received notes of praise from some of the Jamaican lawyers following the case, in particular, Norman Manley, whose congratulatory remarks I greatly appreciated. I began to think, while taking part in this trial, that a lawyer is, in a sense, the most independent sort of person. He is relatively free from attack but free to expose and attack with an unfettered voice which can be used on behalf of a cause.

During the war, local politicians in Jamaica had continued their attempts to win a greater measure of self-government, and in 1944 the Jamaica constitution changed to include a House of Representatives, along with the legislative council, with forty-eight members elected by universal adult suffrage. The way was being prepared for independence, and Manley and Bustamante were in the forefront. My feeling about both men and their parties had not changed. I admired Manley tremendously and felt I would support the People's National Party all the way, but Busta was undeniably the more popular of the two when it came to the masses and I also had great love and warmth for him. He had such genuine affection for people. He liked people and he liked me and invited me to join his party. But I felt he was leading uneducated people nowhere. He was an opportunist, whereas Manley had a programme, a direction which involved education. I told Busta my feelings. He was the sort of man you could sit and talk to for hours. He and his life-long companion and secretary (later his wife), Gladys Longbridge, were always heartily accompanied by good food and drink.

Busta listened to me and said in his broken Jamaican Creole, "When you talkin' to foolish people, foolishness is the best language to use. Education can't stop starvation." He fought well for his people, but simply did not have any policy to speak of. When asked about his foreign policy, he simply said: "We are with the West." That was his terse and famous statement. "We are strongly anti-communist, but I like Castro, he's a great man." That was Busta; he was utterly simple and sincere. Years later as Jamaica's first prime minister, when he met Princess Margaret at Jamaica's independence, he said, "How is yu sista? How is she an' the children?"

That sort of unsophisticated and direct interest in people was so typical of him. Bustamante was the person who drove me nearly fifty miles across the island when my first child, a daughter, was born. Actually, there is an amusing little story attached to it. My wife was not expected to give birth until April, and my sister was expecting a child in March. My sister lived in Panama, and because she was somewhat beyond the normal childbearing age, my mother was worried and wanted me to accompany her to Panama to make sure everything was alright. So I did. My wife was staying in the countryside of Port Maria with her sister, Helen, and brother-in-law, "Buff" Sutherland, and, so as not to agitate her so close to her own time of delivery, I entered into a harmless little conspiracy with "Buff." A certain number of letters had been written and posted from Kingston which he would give to her one at a time over a week so that she would think I was in Kingston and therefore, within reach. Unfortunately, the whole scheme blew up when an airport reporter and photographer took a picture of me leaving for Panama and there it was in the newspaper the next day, a front page picture of me striding in uniform towards the plane. When I came back from Panama, Bustamante was at the airport to meet me. He said, "Get in, you in big trouble," and started to drive with me from the airport. He said, "You're a father," and I kept insisting "No," it was impossible — my wife wasn't due for two more weeks. "Yes," he said, "You're a father and you're in trouble." He drove me all the way to Port Maria and there, to be sure were my wife and my first child, Josephine, born only a few days after I left for Panama.

Busta was at the time Chief Minister of Jamaica and I will never forget the greatness of the man and the personal interest he showed in taking me to see my first born child. Over the years he took a grandfatherly interest in all my children. He attended their birthday parties, and when we visited him, the children would sit on his knee — such a huge, wonderful lion of a man. They must have thought he was Santa Claus. He never failed to offer them a specially picked mango or *othaheite* apple or a piece of sugar cane or some tidbit.

And yet politically I supported Manley. He was an educated man with educated men around him. Where the Black masses thronged to support Busta, it was the middle-class, "brown-skinned," educated people who were attracted to the PNP in the early days. It is a great pity that these two men were divided. The English got between them — "divide and rule" — and the country has been sharply divided ever since. It is a pity because at the time there were no real ideological differences between the two parties, and today the same Black working class is in both parties, bitterly opposing each other. This is the fatality of Jamaican politics: that it is not a class struggle; poor Black people in one party are fighting poor Black people in the other. And neither one of the parties can become so ineffective that they fall further than second place, to wait out their time until the other falls. Parties succeed each other not because one is better, but because the other fails to produce "the goods." The people say "Time for a change, tired of this one, try the other." This has become the present "ten year syndrome" of change. Only in the 1970s did the JLP under Edward Seaga make it clear that it stood for close United States connections, the market economy and free enterprise, while we, under the Manley leadership (Michael Manley, son of Norman Manley), enunciated a clearly different approach, related to central planning, worker participation, and community and self-effort. PNP policy at this point was not to rely on loans from the United States or elsewhere as the main thrust of our economy. But these distinctions did not really reach the masses.

In 1946 I saw an advertisement for the Rhodes Scholarship, and I applied. I knew there were some odds against my getting it: I had not gone through the normal routes of secondary school and High School Certificate Examinations which are general requirements of English colleges. But I was prepared to study and do any catching up that was necessary. The Rhodes Scholarship, as the very highest scholastic award, had never been given to a Black Jamaican, as opposed to a white or "brown" one, and certainly not to anyone who had not made his way through the elite educational system of that time — which meant attending one of the better schools like Munroe or Jamaica College. Mico, as I said earlier, was where poor Black people from the country-parts went for higher education. Though I was somewhat known for my service in World War II, and my defence in the *Bergensfiord* affair, people seemed genuinely surprised when I turned up on the short list for the scholarship interviews at King's House.

Norman Manley was on the committee, himself a prominent Rhodes Scholar, and Bustamante was represented by his Minister of Education. I remember during the interview being asked what I intended to study. I told them frankly that I was not sure, but I had been thinking about studying medicine. The Committee asked me if I was not perhaps interested in becoming a lawyer and Norman Manley said, "There are other ways of healing people besides medicine."

When I won, there were mixed responses. I was elated and honoured, and the first person I ran into after hearing the news was Bustamante. He was having a drink at a bar near Cross Roads and I recognised his car parked outside. I went in and said: "You'll be glad to hear I've just won the Rhodes Scholarship. It will be in the newspaper tomorrow."

He said, "I'm very glad for you son, very glad. What are you going to study?"

I said, "I think I am going to study law."

He replied, "Well you not tall, but you have girth for it."

There were letters written to the newspaper about my being awarded the scholarship. Certain people were outraged: "How can a man like Dudley Thompson represent his country at Oxford?" Others, like Hector Wynter (who wrote a beautiful letter on my behalf in the *Daily Gleaner* and who was chosen as Rhodes Scholar the following year) were adamant in their support. I am of the belief that both Manley and Bustamante played some part in my being chosen.

4 Rhodes Scholar

In 1947 I went back to England as a Rhodes Scholar and entered Merton College at Oxford. My first impression of Oxford was that it was part of old traditional England, but that its quality did not come from being old or traditional, but from the excellence it seemed to expect from everyone. It struck me that it had lasted this long because it never accepted second or third-rate performance. I noticed that I was older than many of the incoming students and I think it made me see the university and my success there in a more mature way. Where many of them at first saw only the form, I could appreciate the grandeur of the place. I had met quite a few people before going there who had "acquired" heavy Oxford accents and I decided that I would take great pains not to acquire one myself while I was there.

I soon discovered that Rhodes Scholars were considered not only the elite among the various colleges, but also the elite of the empire. The queen came to Oxford to meet us. I remember I had recently grown a beard and didn't shave it off for her visit. A number of the scholars were appalled. In the Rhodes House we had a library exclusively for our own use, and there was a Dean of Rhodes Scholars — in my time, an Australian jurist, Dr. C. K. Allen. He and his charming wife generally took care of us, saw to it that we were comfortable, entertained us and kept us in touch with things happening in and around the university. They were a truly delightful couple. We all loved them. In my years at Oxford some of the other scholars included John Bonitto from Jamaica, who became a Wall Street broker and Ken Tynan from Ireland, who later proved himself to be a tremendous literary genius and produced plays at Oxford and in London. There was also Wedgewood Benn, who was to become a leading figure in Britain's Labour Pary; Tony Allyson, a white Kenyan, a talented scholar and close friend — after whom I named my second child, a son, born in England; and David Calder, a white South African with whom I studied, who also went into law. He had a first class brain, a liberal mind and was a good friend. He was clearly destined to go far.

While at Oxford, I also grew closer to some of the West Indian and African acquaintances I had met during the war, people like Kenyatta and Padmore, and soon found myself in a political and intellectual circle which included Kwame Nkrumah, who would be the first president of Ghana, George Lamming, the West Indian novelist, and the eminent historian, C. L. R. James. I became President of the West Indian Students Union and travelled back and forth from Oxford to London, and to Manchester for meetings with students and scholars, and as president I also had close ties with the League for Coloured People (LCP) in London. Founded in 1940 by Dr. Harold Moody, the League came to be considered the conservative darling of British Society. But it had begun as the one place where colonials living in England could air their grievances and protest against colour discrimination, chiefly by means of a regular newsletter which the League published and by its close connection with the Colonial Office. One of the achievements of the LCP was in persuading the Colonial Office to open Aggrey House as a hostel for colonials arriving from overseas. It became home for thousands of students, writers, and others coming to England for the first time. It was through the League that I met Dr. David Pitt, now Lord Pitt, one of the first Black men ever to sit as a member in the House of Lords. When we first met he had just completed his medical studies and was not sure whether he would stay in England or return home to the West Indies. He was always very active politically and gave free medical attention and advice to many West Indian and African students in London and was generally a great advocate on behalf of the West Indian population.

As president of the West Indian Students' Union I often arranged joint meetings and events with our friends in the West African Students' Union. These were not always happy meetings, but proved quite useful. They were designed to bring closer understanding between us but the two groups often revealed strong differences and much ignorance on both sides about each other. This often led to sharp exchanges and some animosity. The Africans often thought the West Indians vain and ignorant of their ancestors' culture. They saw through our (unconscious) desire to imitate the Englishman, our arrogance and blindness towards the advantages of mutual understanding. I sometimes felt the Africans were right and that there was a great need to destroy the inferior status propaganda which had been sown in the West Indian educational system and which looked upon the African as a savage.

I felt it was — and still is — very important to call attention to the blindness and arrogance on both sides; for the reverse was also true: the Africans did not seem to take into account our unique position in history, that we were Africans who had suffered the great ordeal of the Middle Passage — suffered, survived and fitted ourselves to accommodate Western knowledge.

I recall an incident when as liaison officer for the Air Ministry in London, I visited a Royal Air Force station along with a distinguished and high-ranking officer of the Colonial Office, Ivor Cummings. He was Sierra Leonean, of very light complexion, born of an English mother. The West Indians at the station were complaining to us of bad treatment by the English on grounds of colour. After introducing Mr. Cummings as an officer from the Colonial Office who was there to help them, I invited them to tell him their complaints. One tall Jamaican in his Air Force blue uniform, stood up and said on behalf of the others: "Dem treat us jus' like we are Africans, jus' coming out the trees." My friend, Ivor, was enraged. "How dare you?" he exploded. I could hardly resist a smile on seeing the effect of our British colonial education, and apologised to Ivor.

Another organization which had sprung up not long before the war was the International African Friends of Abyssinia which did much to publicize Italy's rape of that country. It had a distinguished group of West Indians and others on the executive committee, including C. L. R. James, Dr. Peter Milliard, T. Albert Marryshow, Jomo Kenyatta, Mrs. Amy Ashwood Garvey, Mohammed Said, Sam Manning and George Padmore. One of the events recorded in connection with IAFA was its welcoming of Haile Selassie at Waterloo Station on his visit to London in 1936. For a short time while the Emperor was in exile in London, the Jamaican writer, Una Marson was his secretary.

The man who brought us all together was George Padmore. He was a Trinidadian-born journalist who had studied at Fisk and at Howard. He first went to Europe with the Black-American Communist, J. W. Ford, to attend the Second Congress of the League Against Imperialism in 1929. There he met British anti-imperialists like Fenner Brockway and soon made the acquaintance of many West Indian and African students in London, including Jomo Kenyatta. Both Padmore and Kenyatta spent some time in Moscow, studying the political situation there, and Padmore also lived in Germany and Belgium where he wrote and distributed pamphlets on colonial issues.

By the time I met Padmore in 1945, he had become a virtual university for all colonial nationalists and for all resistance movements passing through London. Kenyatta, Nkrumah, and Ho Chi Minh were among his disciples. He was a reservoir of knowledge. To listen to him was to see the whole colonial empire unfold before your eyes. He could give details of the party struggle in Cambodia, or the duties of church elders in Barbados, or compare agrarian problems in Jamaica and Tanganyika. Once a member of the Communist Party, he had broken from them mainly because of the Black colonial issue, during the regime of Stalin, and barely escaped punishment. Although his politics included socialism, he was completely dedicated to the idea of Pan-Africanism, which in his words, was "an independent political expression of Negro aspirations for complete national independence from white domination, capitalist or communist."

He was the catalyst in the group of colonial nationalists who met frequently, if not regularly, in London in the late forties. He was one of the most remarkable men I ever met and we remained close friends until his mysterious death in 1959.

I say "mysterious," because I have never received a satisfactory explanation as to how George died. I know that he grew ill in Ghana where he was serving as Kwame Nkrumah's personal advisor on African affairs. I know too that this position aroused great jealously in some of Nkrumah's African friends over there. He was flown from Ghana to London where in the hospital he suffered an internal hemorrhage. I tried very hard, along with Dr. David Pitt, to get closer to his medical attendants in order to find out more about his case. But not even Dr. Pitt, a practising surgeon in London, was allowed to see him. He died and was brought back to Ghana for burial. His grave is in Accra as he wanted it to be. His widow, Dorothy, a Londoner who had been a great worker in the movement and his support and partner for many years, followed him years later and was laid to rest beside him. His death was a great loss to the anti-imperialist struggle. Many of us, especially Kwame, felt a deep personal loss.

George had led a very chequered life as a journalist and political activist. In the early thirties he edited the *Negro Worker* in Germany and was arrested and imprisoned in 1933 by the Nazis for criticising Hitler's racial policies. As a writer some have found him contradictory in his views. He was unflinching, however, in his anti-imperialist outlook and in one of his later books, *Pan-Africanism or Communism?,* he shows his deep commitment to the struggle for the liberation of Africa. To George, colonialism was anathema, and this feeling he passed on to all who came in contact with him.

When I speak of him as a "university," I am thinking of the number of people, especially students, who were influenced by him. He drew like a magnet all Black intellectuals and English Fabians interested in colonial issues to his modest City Council flat near Euston, London. One was never sure whom one might meet there at 22 Cranleigh Street, at any hour of the day or night. It may have been a new African student arriving in England with nowhere to sleep. Beginning on George's couch was an education which would prepare him for the legislature or Judicial Bench in his own country. I happened to be in the presence of George when he got a note from C. L. R. James asking him to meet and look after a young African student, Kwame Nkrumah, who was coming to England. Nkrumah arrived at George's flat, introduced himself — he was an extraordinarily handsome young African — and handed George the letter. George read it, took the pipe out of his mouth and smiled. It was only a few years ago that I found out what was in the letter and why George had smiled. C. L. R. James had written: "The bearer of the letter is Kwame Nkrumah from the Gold Coast. He is determined to drive the British out of Africa and he may well succeed. Postscript — he's not very bright." That turned out to be far from the truth. What C. L. R. James meant by the postscript was that Padmore should take Nkrumah's education into his own hands and not leave it merely to the universities.

People like Ho Chi Minh, Sir Grantley Adams, Dr. Nnamdi Azikiwe, Seretse Khama, Peter Abrahams and Jomo Kanyatta, would spend hours in lively discussion as George with his tremendous library of books, pamphlets and documents unfolded a map of the world and pointed to places as he spoke about them. Together, they would draw up blue-prints for further study and action. It might be Indo-China or the Gold Coast or South West Africa. It was a pleasure to watch George during these discussions. He never lost his cool, or his line of argument. Skillful in debate and eminently knowledgeable, he neither demonstrated arrogance nor unrelenting dogmatism. He listened, followed the discussion and then, when he removed his pipe, his own contribution was adroitly delivered with a smile. I recall how exhilarated he was when he heard that Grantley Adams was coming to Europe to the United Nations to rebut Soviet allegations about Britain's colonial polices. He was to stop over in London en route to Paris, and George was preparing a comprehensive brief for the occasion. He felt that here was a valuable platform to expose the inequities of the colonial system. A few days later he was distraught. In a voice filled with disappointment, he nearly wept as he told me by phone that Grantley had not only departed from an agreed position, but had used a brief prepared for him by the Colonial Office. Padmore felt betrayed. Shortly after this appearance Grantley Adams was awarded a knighthood by the queen of England.

George was a man who understood camaraderie to its fullest extent. He kept the team together. On one occasion when Makonnen, the Pan-Africanist

Ras Makonnen and Josephine Muthoni

George Padmore

restauranteur, was hospitalized in Manchester, George suddenly appeared to interrupt my studies at Oxford and unceremoniously carted me off with him to Manchester. He persuaded Makonnen who lay there very ill in bed to undergo a serious operation and got me to assist him in managing the restaurant during Makonnen's illness. When Makonnen came back some weeks later he found that George had instituted a whole new system of management and had stemmed the flow of loss by theft which had been taking place before. During this whole period George kept up his writing, often typing his column for a Black-American newspaper into the wee hours of the morning.

Nearly everything that I know about the Pan-African movement I learned from George Padmore. Pan-Africanism is essentially an expression of solidarity among Africans and people of African descent. It was originally conceived by a West Indian barrister, Henry Sylvester Williams, practising at the English Bar at the beginning of this century. He had become friendly with many African students while an a law student and had later acted as a legal advisor to several African dignitaries visiting England on political missions. He arranged a Pan-African Conference in 1900 which that great American, W. E. B. DuBois attended. At that time the South Africa Charter Company of Cecil Rhodes was extending its activities into Central Africa, and the ancestral lands of the old African nations were being threatened by both the Boers and the British. The conference in 1900 served as a form of protest against these activities and tried to appeal to the British people themselves to protect Africa. No more than about thirty delegates attended, but as DuBois wrote, it "put the word 'Pan-Africanism' in the dictionary." Williams died eleven years after this conference, but the Pan-African concept was kept alive by DuBois, who organized five international congresses between 1919 and 1945.

I attended the Fifth Pan-African Congress in 1945 while still in the RAF — I had to divest myself of the uniform. The first congress had convened in Paris after World War I while the Peace Conference was taking place and it had aroused much interest among the delegation at Versailles, especially those with interests in Africa. The Fifth Congress which also took place at the end of a great war in Europe, also aroused much interest. Never before had there been such a gathering of Black men and women from all corners of the Empire. This was partly due to the war itself which had pulled so many from the colonies to England to fight and to work in the munition factories.

One noteworthy difference between the first and the fifth congresses was that at the first, Black-Americans wishing to attend had been denied passports. In Padmore's words, "American officials in President Wilson's entourage were afraid that the Congress might discuss, among many things, the lynching of Negroes in the United States and the treatment of Black-American troops in France." In 1945, however, Black-American soldiers who had seen active service in Europe in the Second World War were an important feature of the Fifth Pan-African Congress.

The size and variety of groups attending this congress in 1945 was a culmination of group activities which had been gaining increasing importance in England since the nineteen thirties. One of these groups was the International African Service Bureau whose principal officers were Makonnen, C. L. R. James, and Wallace Johnson of Sierra Leone. They had been giving a series of lectures which attracted both Black and white intellectuals in England. Many, like Padmore, had strong Marxist views at the time and were befriended by the English Fabian Socialists and members of the Liberal Party. At that time, also, Blacks were "fashionable" in certain sectors of European society. Paul Robeson, Josephine Baker and Louis Armstrong were still very much the craze. Nancy Cunard, the American heiress, was a patron of Kenyatta and Padmore and published an article by Kenyatta in her anthology *Negro*. Critics of Kenyatta would later claim that he was a product of the "pink" socialism of England in the nineteen thirties.

One year before the Fifth Pan-African Congress, representatives of various Black organizations had met in Manchester to form a united front. Among them were the Coloured Workers Association from London; the Coloured People's Association from Edinburgh; the United Committee of Coloured and Colonial People's Associations from Cardiff; the African Union from Glasgow and the Association of Students of African Descent from Dublin. This meeting helped pave the way for the 1945 congress. The congress coincided with a meeting of Black labour organizations also held in Manchester that month, and Padmore wrote that one of the distinguishing features of the fifth congress was its "plebeian character." Over two hundred delegates turned up from the Caribbean, Africa, Great Britain and the United States.

DuBois flew from New York to preside over the discussions; he was seventy-three years old at the time. Padmore described this congress as "the coming of age of his [DuBois'] political child." In a sense, it was the coming of age for all of us. For me, taking part in World War II meant taking part in the world; it meant coming out of the dark woods of the colonies and seeing what the empire was really about. And the general feeling running through this congress in 1945 was that the time for action had come.

This congress endorsed the demand for self-government for the people

to escape the press-gangs and the fighting. As a young man he attended meetings of the Kikuyu Citizens Association — the Kikuyu are the largest national grouping in Kenya — and he came to the attention of his people as their natural leader. Anyone looking to the face of Kenyatta could see what I mean by "natural leader." Even as a young man he had the look of a wise old man. Further, he demonstrated great eloquence, dignity and charisma. So much did his own people believe in him that the Kikuyu Citizens Association raised funds for him to be sent to England for further education.

Kenyatta's years in Europe up to the time I met him could fill a book in and of themselves. Among many things, he travelled to Moscow, and also to India where he met and was very impressed and influenced by Mahatma Gandhi. It has always been said, though never proven, that Gandhi awarded him a scholarship to continue his education. He attended lectures at the London School of Economics (LSE) and studied with the well-known anthropologist, Malinowski. Under his tutelage he wrote a series of essays which would later be published as *Facing Mount Kenya*. At LSE he met Prince Peter of Denmark who in turn introduced him to Princess Marie Bonaparte, a great disciple of Freud. She took much interest in Kenyatta, and made a film with him. In the nineteen-thirties he met the young English intellectual Dinah Stock at a rally against imperialism, in Trafalgar Square, and theirs tuned out to be an important friendship. She was secretary of the British Centre Against Imperialism, and had been the first woman at Oxford to chair the Labour Club. She and Kenyatta took an immediate liking to each other and lived together for many years in her flat in London where she diligently worked with him on his writings and political activities. Through her, he met Edna Grace Clarke whom he married in 1942.

Kenyatta, when I met him, was at the point of returning home to Kenya. He went back right after the war and the Fifth Pan-African Conference. He must have simply decided that he had done all that he could in England to acquaint people with his cause. There was never any appearance of urgency about him. Even during the trials of later years of which I would be a part, his demands for his people were simple ones, like better education. He studied his people closely. He was an anthropologist, and he had made it his business to truly understand the ways of his people. To this he added a close understanding of how the English colonial system worked, and he was fearless in challenging it. Of stocky medium height and dignified bearing, he was a born showman, and could fill any stage, always wearing his *kinyatta* and carrying his ornamentally carved African cane. He dwarfed others; and he did this not only by his stature, but by the very wise, patient, almost prophetic look in his eyes. Kenyatta had an imperturbable quality; it was part wisdom and part humour, a gentle outlook rooted in Kikuyu farm life. He would write many years later in *Suffering Without Bitterness:* "I have found joy and humility in the seasonal rhythms. . . . I have seen drought and flood, hail and tempest. I have seen locusts come and crops destroyed by virus or fungus, and livestock stricken by rinderpest or tick-borne disease. One must learn to suffer and endure, to replant and rebuild, to move on again."

He taught me an important lesson in politics, that to be a real leader, you do not so much promote yourself as the people directly under you. You look after the neck and it will always support the head. In his early years of leadership in Kenya, he never suppressed opposition; he encouraged rivals, encouraged leadership in the full confidence that those leaders would support him. And they did. He always looked so much like a tired old wise man that the reverence of others towards him came easily and naturally. He thought before he spoke, then spoke calmly, poetically, using African aphorisms. "Whether the great elephants make love or make war," he once said to me, paraphrasing a Kikuyu proverb, "it is always the grass that suffers." He loved dancing, I remember, especially the African ritual dances. The night before he died he had spent hours dancing. A man of two worlds, he knew the European way of life and understood African culture and gave both full value. The years I spent with him — more importantly, the help I was able to offer him as a friend and lawyer — in East Africa are among the most memorable and important years of my live which I will recount in succeeding chapters.

Friendships made in those early years would prove true and lasting — and would even save lives. One case that comes to mind is when Makonnen, who had gone to Ghana to work with Nkrumah, was arrested during the overthrow of Nkrumah's government. I discovered by pure coincidence, talking to an African visitor who had been my friend at Oxford University and who was on his way as the Ghanaian Ambassador to Mexico, that a mutual friend, T. R. Makonnen, was in serious trouble. Ambassador Akiwe happened to be stopping off in Kingston and came to look me up. We were discussing the recent coup in Ghana and I asked him about Makonnen. He told me that Makonnen had been arrested and was to be executed. I telephoned Kenyatta, who was by then President of Kenya, and by his intervention Makonnen's life was spared.

After I finished at Oxford I spent a year in chambers with Sir Dingle Foot, Queen's Counsel, in London. Foot, who afterwards became England's Attorney General under the socialist government of Harold Wilson, had gained quite a reputation as a barrister in Nigeria, Ghana, Ceylon and other parts of the Commonwealth, and had developed a fair practice before the privy council in London. He was a member of the famous Foot family whose liberal father produced along with Dingle, Michael Foot, noted radical who was recently leader of the Labour Party, and Sir Hugh Foot, to whom I have referred previously in relating the *Bergensfiord* episode. Sir Hugh Foot served as Governor in Jamaica, Nigeria and Cyprus, the last mentioned during the Enosis Emergency.

Having completed my tutelage under Dingle Foot, I began to think about where I would go next to practise. N. W. Manley had invited me to work with him in Jamaica, and I was very flattered by the offer. But I felt if I went back then, the most that would happen was that I would become a rich lawyer. I wanted to broaden my horizons. I wanted to go where there was action. There were other considerations: my infant son had been ill with a number of lung ailments, and Dr. Pitt suggested a change in climate — somewhere dry and elevated and far from the coast. Switzerland was much too expensive, and the other place that came to mind were the slopes of the Kilimanjaro — this seemed very attractive to me, and proved very suitable for my son's health.

Kenya seemed to be the place where the action was about to begin. Padmore encouraged me to go there. We had been getting less and less news from Kenyatta and heard rumours that he was doing poorly. Going back to Kenya, he had become quite frustrated and disappointed, finding no better employment for a man of his calibre and education than reading meters in those European homes and offices that exclusively had electricity. We heard that he was drinking heavily, and Padmore wanted me to go and find out what was happening to him and to his political movement.

All my training had so far been European. I had a strong urge to learn more about the other part of my heritage and it seemed natural that I should go to Africa and live and work there. I decided on the town of Moshi as a place for my family to live. Situated on the lower slopes of the Kilimanjaro in Tanganyika, it is very near the border of Kenya. So in 1951, I set off with my wife and two small children, going on nothing but hope, faith and very little charity. It was one of the most important decisions of my life.

5 MOSHI

We went by boat, the family of four, through the Straits of Gibraltar, across the Mediterranean, and down the Suez Canal, and after a number of weeks along the eastern coast of Africa, we arrived in Mombasa. We feasted on the novelty of a different world. All the women looked like hooded ghosts. They were covered from head to toe in black cloth — all Muslims. There were markets everywhere, filled with beautiful fabrics, ivory, copper, ebony, woven baskets, a tremendous array of colours and warm activity. We took a taxi from Mombasa, which is in Kenya and about two hundred miles from Moshi in Tanganyika. All the Swahili I knew was what I'd learned on the boat from a traveller's brochure, and it was completely inadequate. We stopped at a place called Voi for a meal. It was the only place that resembled a restaurant. Here, we met blank stares from men wearing the traditional fez, a circular tasseled hat without a brim. No one spoke English. To order a meal, I took out a piece of paper and drew an egg, then I drew a chicken. We got fish.

My daughter, who was about five years old, was thrilled with the novelty of her new surroundings. As we passed the different people along the road, we saw Masai with their long spears, resting on one leg, with the other lifted back, so they stood like flamingoes; Wachagga women in long robes and elaborate headdresses. Then of course, the animals — zebras, giraffes, ostriches, gazelles, running in herds and flocks alongside the road in the vast grassland.

In England I had met a Bermudan lawyer named Seaton who had gone out to Tanganyika to practise (he is now Chief Justice of the Seychelle Islands), and I had written to him and made arrangements to stay with him and perhaps work with him for a while. I was not allowed to practise until

I had lived there six months, so I spent the time learning Swahili and the local customs.

We stayed with the Seatons for a short time then moved to a temporary house. I decided not to work with Seaton because it would be too restrictive, being junior partner in a firm where lawyers were so few and far between. I began to meet many local people. V. M. Nazerali, a wealthy Indian who owned sisal estates and most of the cinemas in Tanganyika and Zanzibar, was one of my neighbours. He lived about forty miles away, and our two families became quite close in the year I lived there. I also met the Paramount Chief of the Wachagga, Tom Marealle, of whom I will write more later. He was a handsome, tall African who had been educated in Britain. We became close friends. For the first few weeks he had me terribly confused, introducing me to several women all of whom he called his mother. It turned out that they were all his mothers, in a sense, because of the polygamous marriage custom of the Wachagga people. I also became great friends with an Italian ex-paratrooper who had fought against us in the war. He owned a bar and hotel in Moshi and several houses, and was able to rent us a lovely house. He was great fun and taught me a lot about wines on the evening we spent together on the verandah.

The word *Moshi* means smoke or steam in Swahili. There are innumerable stories as to how the town got this name. One such story is that the region was once actively volcanic and that steam could be seen rising from the craters. What is true, at any rate, is that when I lived there, the town could be distinguished from the surrounding plains in the early morning by patches of smoke slowly rising from the huts otherwise hidden by foliage.

The town centred around the post-office. It was a clean, wind-swept town with a large circular village green of low-cut lawns encircled by purple bougainvillaea perpetually in bloom. Along with the post office there were two banks, Barclays and the Bank of South Africa, facing each other across a narrow road, and a petrol station. The town had no electricity, but there were telephones and electric generators in most offices and European homes. The *boma* was the administrative centre of the district and housed the tax-office and the court house. It was also where the District Commissioner lived. His large attractive house with beautifully kept gardens could easily be distinguished by the flagpole flying the Union Jack in the centre of the lawn.

The busiest, noisiest, most crowded spot in the district was the *sokoni,* or open market. Here, in a babel of languages and a confusion of smells, one could buy fresh vegetables and fruits for next to nothing, not to mention goats, chickens, smoked monkey, termites, caterpillars and various edible barks and medicines. Second-hand European clothes fetched higher prices than the marvelously carved ornaments and woven baskets. You could buy anything there, from bicycles to shoes. It was a strange experience being in this market, which drove me with maddening speed to learn Swahili as quickly as possible. I had learned the Swahili word for "barber" and for "scissors," and also the words *mfupi* for "short," and *mrefu* for "long," and armed with this knowledge I set out to the *sokoni* for my first haircut in Africa. After two or three attempts with accompanying signs I got the message through, and in a babble of well-intentioned replies I was escorted through the market-place, and handed over to an Indian barber. I should have been warned. Either politeness, necessity, or fright made me surrender myself to this man. He literally strapped me into a straight-backed chair in the open, beside the dried shrimp stall which he owned. I say "strapped" because I was swathed in three or four tight layers of very unclean sheeting and could neither rise nor move my arms. My dictionary fell to the ground, and the barber, who had been babbling all the time in some unknown tongue, constantly nodded to show that he understood my two words, *mfupi* and *mrefu.* I could barely move my neck to indicate which part I wanted short, and which long. It was when I saw the blood-stains on the sheet that I knew all was lost. Before I could shout, faint or do something to get someone's attention, the barber stepped away to select from the ground one of the razors which I am sure Vasco da Gama had brought to Africa on his voyage of discovery. He returned with a happy gleam in his eye and from behind gripped my neck in the crook of his arm like a wrestler. A few moments later I felt a cold wind behind my ear. I was being sheared. When, a few minutes later, I was unstrapped and fell out of the chair, I uttered a silent prayer of thanks and dragged myself home. The family was there to greet me and all immediately pointed to my head and laughed. "You should have seen the lion after the tussle," was all I could say to redeem my manhood. After that, I learned the language.

Our house was about two-and-a-half miles from the town. It was a sprawling ranch-type bungalow with a red-shingled roof, very comfortable with all the modern amenities. It was set back about 100 yards from the main road which connects the towns of Moshi and Arusha. This protected us from the heavy dust of traffic in the dry season and the mud for the other half of the year. Our driveway was shaded by a sentinel of large red-blossoming trees — flame of the forest — ending in a circular round-about at the entrance of the house. In the garden, consisting of about two acres of land, we planted roses. The back wall of the living room consisted almost entirely of French doors which opened and closed like an accordion and led to a tiled patio which afforded a breath-taking view of the beautiful Kilimanjaro peak.

The miles of slope between our house and the peak were uninhabited. Now and then we saw groups of graceful giraffe daintily nibbling the tops of acacia trees until they saw themselves being observed. Then they would slowly, with some hauteur, turn to look at us reprovingly, as if we had intruded upon their privacy. We would also hear monkeys chattering away in the trees at the back of the house, and there were teams of zebra and gazelles, often running right across the back of our yard. The servants would call us out and my daughter, Jo, would run out very excitedly to try in vain to "catch" one of the animals.

The mountain herself was a queen, usually concealing her upper portions in layers of cloud. The locals called her *Kibo* and would converse with her. Many a tourist who had traveled miles and waited hours in vain to photograph her peak covered perpetually in snow, would be consoled by his or her local guide: "Kibo does not show her face to everyone." We heard that only "the pure in heart" could see her.

The land seemed so vast when I drove the few miles into town everyday, that I felt as if I was going from everywhere to everywhere. Having been raised in Jamaica, educated in England, and my wife, both raised and schooled in England, we were very much an anomaly in these surroundings. Though racial discrimination was not brazenly practiced here, as in Kenya, I could see at a glance that there were three distinct socio-racial divisions in Tanganyika. The Europeans were at the top of the social ladder. They patronized the two or three European bars attached to the hotels and the "Pink Elephant," a watering hole maintained chiefly for white hunters and their wives. There were a few European women and those that were there kept themselves apart from the Indian or African women. My wife, Pearle, felt somewhat estranged without anyone of similar background or education to talk to, being part-British, part-West Indian. She was considered too "different" from the point of view both of the European and African women. The Indian women also kept very much to themselves. Indians were the businessmen and controlled all the retail and wholesale stores. Their retail shops were called *dukas* from the Swahili, *duka* {s}, *maduka* {pl}, and the less affluent Indians often lived in family compounds surrounding the *duka*. All Indians had African servants living among them, some having been born into the household.

Some Africans were still not used to money or trade. In the town, I often saw a Masai herdsman wandering past the shops and buildings with his cows, on his way to a water-hole. Africans formed a vast backdrop to the other two groups. Many seemed content to go on living harmoniously in the way that their forefathers had, showing little curiosity about European customs. African settlements were usually miles apart. Some, like Marangu, were thousands of feet above sea level, the homes disappearing among the foliage. The Africans also made up the service battalions, the cooks, drivers, nannies and other house servants. We had two servants, Mohammed, the cook, and a young woman who helped in the house and took care of the baby. Mohammed was not only a wonderful cook, he took charge of the household. He kept the house so spotless that I almost felt forced to smoke my cigars outside, and he did all the food shopping. He would, however, take vacations of three weeks to a month, regularly, to attend his "mother's funeral." Eventually I realised that on these occasions he revisited his home region miles away to find himself a new wife with the money he had saved. The Wachagga women were rarely household servants. Men worked, and women were the possessions of men. Marriages were only concluded after payment of so many goats or cows. The donation in fact was the customary dowry paid over to the wife's parents. This custom had much merit as it guaranteed that only the thrifty or hardworking man was entitled to the joys of matrimony.

At first, our greatest difficulty was in fitting into this arrangement of the three races. All social events adhered to the rigid protocol of keeping divided this unholy Trinity: European, Indian, African. It became quite an issue when it was time for my daughter, Jo, to go to school. The best school, the only one suitable, was exclusively European. My wife went to see it and spoke with those in charge, who admitted Jo. After a few days, Jo brought home a letter from the school saying there had been a "mistake." Knowing what the mistake was, I wrote to the governor. He sent back a reply in which he "sympathized" with my family's position, but said that since there were no plans to integrate the school in the near future, admitting Jo would set a "dangerous" precedent. We kept her at home and gave her lessons. After a year in Tanganyika my wife left with the children so that they could be educated in Jamaica.

At that time Tanganyika was a United Nations trusteeship territory, having been a German colony before the war, and the atmosphere was strikingly different to that of Kenya, which was a British colony. In Tanganyika, most of the Europeans were continentals — Italians, Greeks, Danes, Germans; in Kenya, there was a strong contingent of South African whites, Rhodesians and English. In Kenya, law prevented Africans from planting coffee, sisal or other export crops. In Tanganyika there were several wealthy Black citizens, that is, wealthy by African standards. Life in Kenya in the nineteen-fifties was life under apartheid. There was total segregation under the law. Segregation in Tanganyika was more a matter of social custom. The Indian who did not enter the European hotel was not actually prohibited from doing so by a "Europeans Only" sign — which would have been the case in Kenya.

There was a miner, a Canadian geologist, living in the area, whose name was Williamson. He was a very heavy drinker and had fallen on bad times. His African mistress looked after him with the tender care of a good wife. He had three interests — whisky, his woman and geology. He was nearly always drunk and always penniless except when some kind friend lent him a small sum to carry on. Often, his woman had to carry him home from the bars, and when he went into the mountains prospecting, that is searching for minerals, she went with him. She had no difficulty getting food from friends. They were a well-known couple, among the Europeans as well as the Africans. There was an especially kind friend, the Scottish wife of a wealthy Indian lawyer. From time to time, Mrs. Chopra would lend Williamson a thousand shillings or so. One evening he visited the Chopras for the usual "handout." Mr. Chopra, fed up, remonstrated with his wife for encouraging laziness. She however, kind soul, could not let him down and dropped a small note to her banker in the town of Mwanza. It was late and although the banks were closed, he was given the money. Williamson thanked her and left.

On the way home with his woman, the donkey, and their pack, they went into the mountains to do some more prospecting. After this trip, Williamson never had to ask for anything the rest of his life. He discovered what are now the Williamson diamond mines in Tanganyika. He never forgot his friends. Mrs. Chopra received from time to time as a gift of thanks, specially selected diamonds. Mr. Chopra got a percentage in the mines and was retained as lawyer at a handsome fee. Williamson built a lovely modern house on Lake Victoria and had it comfortably furnished for his woman. She had a car and chauffeur which she rarely used. At first she enjoyed the radio and had one in almost every room, but soon grew tired of the new life and preferred the old days when he had spent more time with her. Now he was busy flying here and there as the mines developed. Her happiest moments, I was told, were when her African friends came to visit her.

Williamson, by nature a philanthropist, gave much of his wealth to charity, especially African causes. He tried, in vain, to fight the De Beers South African diamond monopoly and failed. Eventually he drank himself to death, dying of a bad liver. The Williamson story could never have taken place in Kenya.

After a few months of settling down in Tanganyika, I traveled across the White Highlands of Kenya to see and visit Kenyatta. To travel across the White Highlands of Kenya and see the sleek zebra or full grown lion stalking him, was to imagine the Garden of Eden. Most of the vast land had never been tilled. The extensive European farms were miles from each other and consisted of large sprawling acres of the best land in Kenya. The Kikuyu, on the other had, were crowded into small patches here and there which they owned as a community. There, they eked out a living with primitive tools from the grudgeful earth, and were often visited by famine, locusts and drought. Many had no alternative but to join the gangs of indentured labourers on the European farms. Many of these labourers were brought to the farms in sealed trains, really ox-wagons, from Nyasaland or the Congo (now Malawi and Zaire respectively). They lived and worked unconscionable hours on these farms which produced the best coffee in Africa and whose thoroughbred herds of cattle were magnificent to behold. The background of African discontent was always the unfair distribution of land and the labour legislation which ran parallel with it. My early work as a lawyer in Kenya usually involved assisting the Kikuyu in legal battles over land.

Of all the people in Kenya, the Kikuyu had been most affected by European settlement. At the beginning of the century, Europeans had entered Kenya with the intention of turning the central highlands into an exclusively white area. By the nineteen-thirties terms such as "White Highlands" and "White man's country" had come into use when describing Kenya. The Masai and the Kamba were herdsmen. The Masai in particular were nomadic and so their lives were not greatly changed when Europeans began growing coffee in the highlands. The Kikuyu, however, had always lived off the land as farmers. They had, in fact, a mystical attachment to their land. This partly derived from a myth in which the Creator bestowed miles of highland and forest on the father of the tribe, Gikuyu. Not only were they herded into restricted areas; they were also prevented from growing lucrative cash crops. It was by doing this that the Europeans were able to turn the Kikuyu into an agricultural proletariat — a dependable source of labour for farmers.

On the other hand, because the Kikuyu were in closest contact with the Europeans, they took advantage of the education provided by missionaries. So it is no wonder that it was the Kikuyu who would lead the national liberation struggle. I began meeting Kenyatta frequently on his cattle-farm outside Nairobi, and also in the city where he held meetings of the KAU — the Kenya African Union.

Nairobi is a large, beautiful, modern city. It was a great pleasure, after the long dusty ride, to see the high-rise buildings and clean wide streets with traffic divided by islands of bougainvillaea.

Politically, this is how Kenya was constituted. There were fifty-four members in the legislative council. Thirty-six were European and all elected; twelve were Asian, with six elected and six appointed by the governor; and there were six Africans, all appointed by the governor. In this sense, the African people had no vote, no voice in the government. There was also a system of appointed chiefs — appointed by the colonial government.

Sometimes an appointed chief such as Koinange, who was a traditional chief from an old ruling family, was genuinely concerned about his people, but often it was a case of a "preferred" African, someone who would collaborate with the Europeans in keeping firm control of the African population.

Kenyatta, with my support and legal help, was advocating a system of land registration for Africans. Many of the Africans did not understand that this would help them. Traditionally, the chiefs "owned" all the land in the designated African areas, but because it was not registered, Europeans could at any time confiscate it. It was over a case of confiscated land that I came to know chief Koinange, one of the greatest Africans in Kenya at that time.

It was 1952, and I had lived in East Africa for a year. By then news had traveled by word of mouth among the Africans that there was a Black lawyer practising in Moshi. There were of course, educated Africans like Chief Marealle and Kenyatta who knew me well, but among the ordinary Africans who did not understand the law, there grew a certain curiosity tinged with respect for the African from a strange land, namely myself, who would advocate on their behalf in the courts. How Koinange and his family came to know of me, I am not sure, but one day in 1952 they traveled over one hundred and fifty miles from the village of Kiambu in Kenya, to seek my help.

He was brought to my house by some of his sons and other Kikuyu, all of who treated him with the greatest reverence. He was in his eighties by then, wizened as a prune and impeccably dressed in European clothes with starched collar, and shining cuff-links. He was completely bald, every inch of his skin wrinkled (some of my African friends used to say the Koinange had been born one year after God; he seemed so old) but his eyes were piercing and clear. He was the Paramount Chief of the Kikuyu, imperious without being arrogant. When people opened doors for him or showed their respect in other ways, he accepted it simply and with dignity as his right as senior chief. He was truly the last of the great chiefs of that people. His father had been senior chief, as had his grandfather, and so on as far back as Adam, I believe. His own life had spanned the years before colonization, and he recalled the first white men to come to his district. Koinange gave me an almost picturesque description of his first contact with those foreigners. They had wandered into Kikuyuland. They had been poor and hungry and his father, an old patriarch, had given them food. The food, he said, had consisted of goat's meat and milk and he had sent men into the trees for wild-honey. Koinange did not speak a word of English, not even "yes" or "no." This is my own translation of his story as I remember it, narrated to me entirely in Swahili:

"It was early in the morning and the mist was just rising from the valleys. The grass was fresh and green. The young men, who had just gone out with the herds, returned to say that strange men and women, with a few small children, had been seen nearby. They had no *manyatta* [home] and seemed to be foraging for food. They were strange people and did not belong to any known tribe. Their skin was white. They spoke a strange tongue and their dress was strange. When the Chief [Koinange's father] sent the men back to invite the leaders of this strange tribe to meet him, he sent gifts of honey, goat meat and sweet potatoes. The pink-faced people came, wearing strange clothes which followed the shape of their bodies [trousers]. They had nothing and the chief let them stay on a portion of the land.

"Little by little they took more land from us and today we cannot even walk on the roads outside their houses."

This was a plaintive cry straight from the heart of Africa, from one of her sons looking back in his own lifetime at the exploitation of his people under the colonial system. Koinange was later prosecuted for growing coffee on this land. He had long complained, on behalf of his people, about the unfair distribution of land. In 1936 he had written to the governor, warning him that the African people did not like to be removed from the land which held the graves of their ancestors and that to do so was for the African "to be suddenly torn in their spiritual body." He fearlessly went on to say that if the government did not change its policies, "people might become disobedient."

Unlike some of the other paramount chiefs, Koinange took his position as head of his people in earnest. His was a patriarchal role. As father of his people he settled disputes and no one was refused food or sustenance in his house. Whenever there was calving or a special bumper crop, a portion of the animal or harvest was set aside for him, and on his visits to a district there would usually be a feast. I attended many of these feasts with Koinange, and I witnessed the procession of men and women who brought him gifts. All property, including land, was held by him in trust for his people. Now he wanted me as a lawyer to defend not only his rights, but the rights of all his people to their own land. Ironically, he had great faith in the British crown and in the Houses of Parliament in England. Yet it was Koinange who became the first great target for oppression by the British ruling class in Kenya. They could not understand the great hold, the mystical reverence, which he engendered among his people, who numbered over one million. I will never forget the deference shown to him by the Africans who accompanied him, and indeed, of all Africans in his presence. They bowed to him before speaking and after hearing his replies. It was respect for the man himself, not fear or awe of his title. He was undeniably the most fearless defender of his people's interests and the most revered of African chiefs.

That same year as court proceedings dragged on about the confiscation of his people's lands, Koinange made a moving speech at an important political gathering of Africans in Kiambu: "In the First World War you asked our young men to go fight with the British against the Germans and many were killed. In the Second World War you came again and asked us to fight against the Germans and the Italians and our young people were again ready to go. Now there are Italians and Germans in Kenya and they can live and own land in the highlands from which we are banned, because they are white and we are Black. What are we to think? I have known this country for eighty-four years. I have worked on it. I have never been able to find a piece of white land."

Koinange was found guilty of growing a prohibited crop, ordered to pull up all the coffee plants on his land, and heavily fined. He appealed to the Kenyan Court of Appeal, but lost. Still, Koinange persisted. He insisted that there be an appeal to Her Majesty's Privy Council in England. He had an abundance of faith in the British system of justice. Most Africans would not have had either the courage or money to carry the issue this far. Koinange sold a saw mill and some buses he owned, to cover the legal expense. The result was that the Privy council overruled the Kenya Court of Appeal on the grounds that the legislature had exceeded its powers and had no right to pass a law intrinsically against the interests of the native people, and that it was flagrantly against their colonial policy. It was a triumph for British justice and for Koinange. But the Kenyan government would not forget their defeat and Koinange would be singled out later during the Mau Mau state of emergency.

Koinange's was an exceptional case, but there were other instances where I had to appear on behalf of the Africans in Kenya. Koinange's son, Mbiu, often needed help against the authorities. Mbiu had been educated in the United States at Columbia University. Returning to Kenya, he established the Kikuyu Independent Schools. This was violently opposed by the European community on various grounds: e.g., "inferior" teaching, "unsanitary" conditions and that Kikuyu rather than English was being emphasized. Mbiu's schools were constantly being closed down. Yet the schools had not received a single penny from the government. The Africans, under the direction of the chiefs, had built the schools themselves. They had provided their own teachers and taught Kikuyu history and folklore, as well as fundamentals like reading and writing.

Mbiu began a teacher training college at Githunguru and offered the position of Vice Principal to Kenyatta. Kenyatta had married one of Koinange's daughters and in this way had become part of this leading Kikuyu family. After the first signs of Mau Mau activity (raids on European farms in which cattle were maimed) the government linked Kenyatta's position at Githunguru with that of his position as head of the Kenya African Union, and in a report to the government, the district commissioner stated that the Mau Mau, the KAU and the Kikuyu Independent Schools were "all the same old stiffs working under different guises in order to increase the number of public meetings." Kenyatta, the entire Koinange family and those affiliated with the teacher training college were kept under government surveillance.

One day I was visiting Kenyatta at Githunguru. We sat in the garden under a tree, and were talking about the completion of one of the school's buildings when it was announced that a woman had arrived and wanted to see him. She was waiting at the bottom of the hill. He told the messenger to bring her up. She was bearing a large stone tied to her back. It was limestone cut neatly with square corners. She bowed to Kenyatta and they spoke together, not in Swahili, but Kikuyu. I noticed that she was barefooted and dressed in the traditional dress with one shoulder bared. After a while, she unloaded the stone. I could see that Kenyatta was very pleased. He turned to me smiling: "Dudley, this woman walked over forty miles to bring me this stone. Her name is Elizabeth. She is offering me the stone to build a college for women. She herself is illiterate. She says she wants me to build it so that when our men go abroad to be educated they do not come back with English wives. She says they are being educated away from their tribe and their women. This stone is her contribution and she wants to organize the women in her district, each one to bring a stone to build the college."

This was the spirit of the Kikuyu as I knew them in the early fifties. They were people who were taking their future into their own hands in a peaceful and hard-working manner. It was these same people who would be described within a few years by those imposing the state of emergency, as "savages insatiable for blood."

As I drove the many miles between the towns of Kenya and Moshi, I would often think about Jamaica. I would think particularly about the difference between our Black peoples. And as I approached that little town nestling in the foothills of the Kilimanjaro, I would see my own people, of Kingston, or Darliston, in an unusually clear light. We had left behind all but a trace of our Africanness. The cultural chain had been utterly severed. A descendant could not understand a single word of the ancestor's language. We had, worst of all, not only a lack of appreciation for our ancestral culture, but had been taught to disdain it. Our progress had depended upon how near we came as carbon copies to the original — the original in this case being English. Time was to prove that the West Indian could imitate so well that he exceeded the master in many fields — cricket for example. The English taught us the game and today the West Indies team, since the captaincy of Barbados' Garfield Sobers, has been indisputably the best in the world.

I often imagined, driving though Moshi and past the villages and the crowded *masoko,* that it was an appropriate time for other West Indians to come to Africa, to feel the great pulse of the people from whom we had descended, and to help pass on the skills we had learned by being part of the West. I tried to put such a plan into action by writing to friends in Jamaica and the newspapers. I envisioned a team of lawyers, teachers, engineers and other professionals from the West Indies spending several years in Tanganyika as I was doing. I got few responses. It would be years still before Jamaicans felt a great need to bridge the gap between themselves and their African past.

Tom Marealle, Paramount Chief of the Wachagga in the area around Moshi, became one of my closest friends while I lived in Tanganyika. Tom had been nurtured and trained by the British for his role as chief. Part of his training was in Welsh, a language hardly more widely known that Wachagga. The greater part of this training, however, consisted in living with English families, chiefly ex-civil servants, in the hope the "poor frightened fellow" would be indelibly impressed with the superior British way of life.

He was a shrewd but amiable man, and we lived very closely together. He thoroughly enjoyed his position, and friends referred to him as "King

Tom." He was a well-built man, just over six feet. His smile came easily. He spoke English beautifully, and he oozed charm. He was a great lover. Few African women were ever expected to tell him "no." There was one exception, however: a very outstanding woman of whom I will speak later.

Among the Wachagga, Tom's word was law; but, in truth, he was a ceremonial ruler among a peaceful and orderly people He had little to do other than visit the outlying villages, and often I accompanied him and enjoyed the feasts prepared for him. When the three or four cars (Tom, myself and others in his retinue) drew up on these occasions, we were met by his chiefs or sub-chiefs, all wearing colourful robes and feathered head-dress. Tom wore a tall plumed helmet, and a black and white belt, both of Colobus monkey fur. Over his European clothes he wore two full pelts of the leopard and carried either an ornately carved cane of ivory or a beautifully beaded fly whisk of giraffe tail hairs. He would offer his hand to be kissed, and accepted it naturally as people prostrated themselves before him. *"Mshimbuye,"* they would say ("Welcome, anointed one"). And he would reply: *"Baraka —mungu saida"* ("Blessings, God be with you"). Then he would introduce me, and we would take our seats at the table on which there would be whisky, gin, other drinks, and huge chunks of goat meat, hot from the spit. The goat would have been specially reared and fattened for Marealle. He would call up the chief or sub-chief, converse with him a bit about the village, then offer him some special part of the meat such as the loin. The chief would proudly accept the honour and return to his place, then Tom would repeat this with other elders in turn, all of whom were glad to be acknowledged by name. He would repeatedly refer to me throughout the feast as his friend and brother and accepted member of the tribe. This, like everything he said, would be greeted with smiles and acclamation.

Then the serious eating and drinking began. Long strips of meat would be cut away from animals roasted whole and hanging from hooks. Young girls, bare-breasted, brought out basins of water and towels. They smiled shyly as Tom spoke to them, curtseyed, and then ran off giggling, flattered to have met him, and disappeared into the surrounding homes or joined the dancers who entertained us while we ate. Later the men would do their own dance with spears and shields and painted faces. These dancers usually wore tall ostrich plumes in their hair, and tied conch shells or balls round their ankles which rattled as they stamped their feet in unison. It was altogether a menacing performance, put on to impress their friends and to display the ferocity with which they would defend their chief.

There were fifty or sixty such villages in Tanganyika's northern province.

In towns like Voi and Tanga, which were among the largest, these festivities or *siku kuu* took on a more formal aspect. Leading members of the administration, the British as well as leaders of the Indian community and a few Arabs, would be invited as guests of honour. The people prepared for them some days in advance. The beating of drums was heard for miles away as the guests approached the site of the festivities. All through the feasting there would be incredible singing and drumming. It is hard to describe the spontaneous spirit of pleasure emanating from such a crowd. The feast would go on all day and night — getting more spirited in the later hours after most of the distinguished guests had gone, and much alcohol had been consumed — bare skins moving for hours in the moonlight to the magic, hypnotic rhythm of the drums.

Marealle had a council centre, a beautiful modern town hall built for him near his official residence. Over the entrance was an expensive coat of arms hewn from Carrara marble imported from Italy. The idea of the centre (along with the modern two-story residence with its graceful columns, wide verandah and flag-pole in the circle of the driveway) reflected the policy and life-style of the British district commissioner. Tom enjoyed it, but politically it set him too far above his people and their customs. When Tom visited the larger homes of his sub-chiefs and they sat on the ground eating with their fingers, talking Kichagga, I sensed an entirely different atmosphere, one of traditional camaraderie.

The tribe was a family, with the chief as its father. Everyone else was an outsider. I recall one occasion when I was asked by a member of the Wachagga to defend his son who had been charged with murdering one of his wives. I visited the prisoner who was in a jail some seventy miles away. The first question put to me, by the accused, was *"Kabila gani?"* ("What is your tribe?"). I replied: "African." He arrogantly responded *"Sijui"* ("I do not know that tribe"). It was difficult for him to understand why a stranger should try to help him.

There were many differences in custom, language and food among the national groups. Though the Moslem influence was strong and there were far more schools teaching the Koran than the Christian Bible, animists outnumbered both Moslems and Christians, and the *mchawi* or traditional teacher was a power not to be crossed. Many Africans, and the *mchawi* in particular, had great knowledge of herbs, including poisons. The Wandorobo lived in the mountains and were rarely seen in the towns. They used blow-pipes for hunting, and killed even elephants with their poison darts. Remote groups like these were completely cut off from the rest of Africa. They knew nothing other than daily happenings within their own immediate surroundings.

It was always a pleasure to see someone from one of the lesser-known tribes such as the Wandorobo suddenly wandering into the town, or to see them moving through the plains as I drove along the great highways. To see a Wandorobo dressed in animal skins — or a Masai — was to be reminded of a whole other Africa. The Masai refused to live anywhere but in the open. Their faces had an extraordinarily peaceful expression, yet they could kill with swift calm precision. The Masai could stride for miles with a graceful lope which combined a grace and dignity beautiful to behold. They had been lion hunters for centuries and could kill lions with a single thrust of a spear. Their bodies were smeared with a special mud which gave their skins an incredible red hue, and they lived on only the milk, blood and meat of the cow. There was a drink the Masai made from the blood and milk of their cattle. I remember being offered this once and wondering if I would survive the ordeal. I looked at the circle of Masai herdsmen around me, tall, strong men, and decided it hadn't killed them, it wouldn't kill me. The Wachagga had a similar drink which I was offered and again drank just as unwillingly. It was call *kissusuyu* and was made from the blood and milk of goats. They cut the vein of the goat and let the blood pour into a calabash or bowl, then it would be whisked vigorously so as not to curdle, while it was warmed on an open fire. Often they removed a thin layer of fat from the slaughtered goat and this they wrapped, like a piece of cellophane, round pieces of raw flesh and entrails so that it formed a sort of sausage. The whole thing was then dropped into the blood and was ready to be served almost raw and only slightly warmed. They had no seasonings, and salt was very precious and rarely used.

I visited Marealle often, almost daily. We met and drank or ate together. Sometimes we talked about serious matters, but often about social affairs. To the women, he was a prize to be sought; to him, they were a pleasure befitting a paramount chief. On one occasion he consulted me about a suggestion which had been made to him by the district commissioner. The district commissioner had suggested that Tom introduce identity cards among his people to prevent infiltration by the Kikuyu on the border. At this time, trouble between Kikuyu and government had begun in Kenya. I realised that these identity cards would benefit no one but the Europeans. Machagga could easily identify any Kikuyu among them, and vice versa. I advised Marealle strongly against it, pointing out that it was the beginning of the Pass Laws as in South Africa. He was in complete agreement with me, and it was one of the few incidents in which he showed resistance to the administration.

On another occasion I went to Marealle for advice and assistance. Along with my assistant, a young Wachagga man who acted as my secretary, I needed someone who could speak both Kichagga and Swahili, English of course, and perhaps some Kikuyu. He said: "That would be hard — I don't know of any such person." He was pensive for a while and went into a hammock where he lay thinking. Finally he said, "There is one person — a girl." He paused, "But I would strongly advise against hiring her." When I asked why, he was very evasive. My curiosity was completely aroused. "What's wrong with her, Tom?"

"She's a very different kind of person," he kept repeating.

"Is she honest, reliable, trustworthy?" I asked.

"Yes," she was all these things, he said, but repeated his warning: "She is trouble."

Finally, I found out from him that the woman — who I will call Flora — had once lived in Moshi, but was now living in Tanga with a Swiss doctor who had left his wife for her. She had been trained as a nurse, but was no longer working at the hospital. She sounded perfect for the job. Tom, however, seemed quite put off by the very thought of her, so I dropped the subject.

Weeks later I was travelling to Dar es Salaam by train — quite an experience. To escape the noisy, perspiring crowd with their baggage, bicycles, chickens, baskets, babies, bundles and fruit, I went first-class. My fellow-traveller was an Indian prison-warden in officer's uniform. After some miles we struck up a friendly conversation in Swahili. Hearing that I was from Moshi, he asked: "Do you know Flora?" I was very surprised. "No," I replied. "Do you?" "Oh!" he replied, and rolled his eyes in admiration. "Tell me about her," I said. "She is different," he said. "Different from African women." He told me that she was working in Tanga, and as the train stopped for some time there on its way to Dar es Salaam, I decided to get off and look for her. By this time I was completely intrigued.

I got a taxi at the station and asked to be driven around the town as I'd never been there before. While being driven I told the driver I was looking for a woman named Flora. He nodded, revealed a knowing smile and, in a flurry of language completely incomprehensible to me, quickly took me to a house. It took me about five minutes to accustom my eyes to the darkness inside this house, as he spoke to the well-dressed woman who had approached us with a mug of beer, and who spoke in a language unknown to me. I paid her for the beer and sipping it, I tried to explain to the driver that there had been some mistake. The driver and the woman spoke, and then the woman disappeared behind a colourful screen and reappeared with two much younger beautiful African women. They both wore nothing above the waist, and diaphanous silky pantaloons gathered at the ankles with wide silver bracelets. I had great difficulty leaving, but managed to get back to the car!

After two more similar stops, I mentioned to the driver that this Flora was a nurse. He seemed immediately to recollect, knocked his palm against his forehead and drove me to a house on the outskirts of Tanga. There, he spoke to a rather buxom, pleasant-looking woman who, after a few minutes, invited me out of the car into her house. The house was furnished in European style, that is, there were curtains in the glass windows, a calendar and prints on the walls. There was also a coffee-table with framed photographs. She offered me a drink which I declined, saying I had to catch a train. She turned out to be Flora's sister — the real Flora — and asked me the purpose of my visit. I explained that I had never met Flora but that she had been highly recommended and I wanted to interview her for a job as my secretary, having explained that I was a lawyer who lived in Moshi. She showed me a photograph of Flora and I knew at once that this was the person I had been looking for. She was different.

I could see from the photograph that she was exceptionally beautiful. I left, hoping Flora would receive my message and come to Moshi. The whole experience had moved me — the picture, the search, the chance of meeting her.

A few weeks later, Melchizedek, my clerk, came into my office. He was both clerk and confidante. Well-paid, he let me into many secrets and local nuances which otherwise would have escaped me. He announced, in his usual way, that there was someone to see me, a woman. "Send her in," I answered routinely. He moved to do so, then returned and sat down. In almost apologetic confidence he said to me, "It's not an ordinary client. It's Flora. She's a very different type of person." I asked: "What is so different about her?" He shook his head and said that he couldn't explain; she was different from other women, he said. "Send her in," I said again, determined once and for all to get to the bottom of this mystery.

She came in — or rather bounced in with a springy step — and extended a slender hand which I shook warmly. Then she sat facing me with a smile of total confidence revealing perfect teeth and dimples. She really was quite attractive, though badly dressed in European clothes, a see-through blouse and a too-tight revealing skirt that did severe injustice to her body. She led the conversation: "I heard that you wanted to see me. My sister said you came to Tanga. I am sorry I was not there but I was attending to my goats."

"Goats?" I asked.

"Yes," she smiled again, "I own many goats in Tanga where I live."

I really didn't know how to begin; I was completely surprised. I think I said, "I'm a lawyer working here in Moshi and need someone to assist me in my office. Do you think you can do the work?"

She said, "Oh yes, I am sure." She spilled over with confidence.

"I'm not sure you will like it. It's very different from tending goats. It will mean leaving Tanga to live here in Moshi."

She said, "I know I will like it — my mother lives here in Moshi. When would you like me to start?"

My natural caution suddenly told me to go more slowly. I sat back and began to study her. Her English was faulty, but reasonably good and she showed not a trace of the usual shyness of most African women. "How are you so sure you can do the job?" I asked.

Her reply was a clincher: "What I don't know, I will learn," and, she added, "I have heard what you are doing for my people."

I told her to start Monday morning, a few days ahead.

I realised over the next several weeks, why everyone called her "different." Aside from her beauty and outstanding intelligence, she had a unique air of independence which made her unlike any other African woman I had met. African men, Marealle included, simply did not know what to make of her. It is not surprising that this woman was later given an important position in the government of independent Tanzania. Her ambition and aptitude for learning new skills was awe-inspiring. She stayed in my employment for almost all my remaining years in Tanganyika. After a few weeks I got to know her sufficiently well to advise her not to wear such revealing clothes. In a country where nudity went unnoticed there was no half-way course — you either wore African or European attire. She took my advice, although at her mother's home she reverted to more comfortable African dress — barefoot with a single floral cotton wrap tucked under her arms. She was happiest then: her unique laugh, loud and resonant, would fill the house. She enjoyed correcting my linguistic mistakes and introducing me to new African foods. I bought a used Underwood typewriter from an Indian and taught her to type. Daily, Africans came to the office and stood for hours looking through the window at the African woman using a typewriter. To them, typists were always Indian or European. Flora enjoyed her new status. She knew they thought her "different" and she lived up to it. Later, she became the first African woman in that district to get a driver's license, and later still after much wrangling with the District Commissioner, she got a passport. Meanwhile she brought me up-to-date on local political and social life. It always amused me that Marealle never showed any interest in her, considering she was so strikingly beautiful. I recall more than one

European exclaiming at her exceptional beauty upon first seeing her. It was this same Flora who later became an early member of the government with TANU — the ruling party which brought the country to independence in 1961.

One Friday afternoon Melchizedek announced that there was a gentleman outside my office who had been waiting to see me. Apparently he had been sitting for some time, allowing others to precede him. He came in, a small thin gentleman, very pleasant and soft-spoken. He seemed grave, though he wore a smile beneath his Chaplin moustache. His English was not only perfect but rang with politeness.

He introduced himself as Julius Nyerere, a school teacher from Dar es Salaam. He had heard of my law practice and had come for some advice. I asked him how much time he had to spend in Moshi. He said he had planned to stay no longer than one day, but could stay longer if necessary. I invited him to come home with me and to spend the weekend with my family. On the way home I got more acquainted with him and was charmed by him at once. There is no other way to describe our meeting. We spoke of many things that evening, during dinner, after dinner, at breakfast the next day, and thereafter. He told me of his political aims and drive for independence. My advice to him was "organize, organize, organize." And he received the advice with some relief. I was merely confirming a decision he had already made.

I was impressed with his very realistic and yet far-reaching vision which stressed the political education of his people. An ardent Catholic, the father of five children, trained at Edinburgh University as a teacher, he has always remained a teacher. Today he is affectionately called *"mwalimu,"* which means "teacher," and was called that throughout his presidency.

Nyerere had already decided to form a political union to work towards independence. His idea was to make it exclusively African, and I argued against this at first, wanting to include several liberal Indian and European friends who would have been glad to donate the funds which we would need. He rejected the suggestion. "It must be purely African — our effort." The Tanganyika African National Union, or TANU, was to have branch headquarters in every town. I must confess that when he left at the end of that weekend, I had no idea that Nyerere's will and dedication would develop quite as they did.

His was a dedication and singleness of purpose which would have a snowball effect throughout the whole territory. It gathered strength as a small flame and rose like the sun over the Kilimanjaro to spread its warmth and strength over people long separated by language and custom. I realised that a peaceful revolution was about to take place. After returning to Dar es Salaam, he continued with his meetings. Nyerere continued organizing the party along the lines he had discussed. Some time after our first meeting an incident occurred which by itself was not so unusual but turned into a political opportunity which Nyerere maximized to its fullest potential.

The Tanganyika government, acting under pressure from European farmers, decided to remove the entire Mwarusha people from the Arusha region — a coffee-growing region known for its perfect, mild, healthy climate — and to distribute the land among some European farmers. The Mwarusha refused to go. They were promised better lands elsewhere, but still they refused. They were told that they had overgrazed their land and that the cattle would die, but they remained adamant about staying. Eventually they were forcibly removed by the police, who put them in trucks and transported them miles away. They walked back and squatted on their old lands. The police then set fire to their huts. The Mwarusha dug trenches and slept in them. Nyerere took up their cause and came to Moshi for my legal advice.

He decided that he would present the people's case at the highest level. He took it to the appropriate committee of the United Nations in New York. Nyerere's presentation had such a dramatic and telling effect that the Colonial Office decided to send the governor to argue against it. Sir Edward Twining submitted that any move towards independence at that stage would be a retrograde step, leading to chaos and inter-tribal squabbling. He said that he did not see the country gaining independence within his lifetime. It took eight years to prove him wrong. Nyerere was a complete success abroad, not only at the U.N. but at the meetings of various influential groups that he attended. At last he had found a platform which at that time seemed more adequate to his political dimensions.

His return found him working harder than ever. The government tried to turn some of the chiefs against him, and there were some who considered Nyerere an upstart, someone who threatened their own status. But the undercurrent of popular support was strong.

Since political education was the first step, I had tried to help by organizing meetings at the district level in Moshi. I helped to resuscitate the Wachagga Citizens Association which had been started by an old aspiring politician named Petro Njau. When I had first come upon it, it was a dying group of people whom I had invited to hold weekly meetings under the trees in my garden. Petro had been among the first group of Wachagga to be sent by the Germans to Berlin for an education — before the war when Tanganyika had been a German colony. The group, now led by both of us, began taking on a new life. The fifteen or twenty elders who used to attend out of habit suddenly grew to two hundred, then three and four hundred, and kept on increasing. The meetings took the most elementary form of political education and were carried on entirely in Swahili.

After the gathering had sat down on the grass, the elders in front in their traditional dress, I would come out of the house with an assortment of books, magazines, photographs and maps. I would stand and greet them: *"Jambo,"* or more correctly *"Hamjambo,"* and they would reply *"Jambo Bwana,"* raising their right hand in a respectful salute. I realised that these meetings had aroused the attention and suspicion of government authorities, and that informers were always present. To be sure the opening ritual, when reported, must have taken on frightening proportions. After the salute, I would bend down and in my fingers grasp some loose earth, then, straightening up, let it fall slowly through my fingers as I intoned in Swahili: "This is our land. It belonged to our ancestors. Anyone who tries to take it from us is evil and must be resisted." This, they all repeated solemnly.

Then we began the lesson for that day — the meeting always began about noon and went on until the sun quietly followed its rays behind the snow-capped Kilimanjaro. The lessons were rudimentary — pictures and stories about kindred people in the West Indies and America. But I felt that somewhere in that ocean of hungry minds, the minds of men who wanted to regain the ancient position of self-respect in their own land, perhaps a pebble was cast. And the ripples would go out wider and wider until time and patience had completed the picture. It was my plan that this fruitful organization would eventually be turned over to Nyerere, and I discussed this with Petro Njau.

Petro was a remarkable person. He always wore European clothes and carried around papers of some sort in his hand. He wore steel-rimmed spectacles and a hat which completely covered his bald head. The few remaining hairs on his head were white. His smile was constant. I believe he slept with it. He was always ready to learn, and usually I introduced an idea as if it had come from him. Then he would speak for hours, thoroughly enjoying the burgeoning of "his" idea. I was able to put succinctly into words, all the things that were "his own dream."

Marealle once had a celebration to mark the opening of the largest building in Tanganyika. It was the Kilimanjaro Native Cooperative Union Headquarters — an impressive structure with a roof-garden for entertainment and social functions. The building had been financed by a windfall of the African coffee planters, who had obtained a fourfold increase in price because of an unusual frost in Brazil. Instead of allowing the individual planters to receive a bonanza and spend it on cars and luxuries, Marealle, realizing that the bonanza was unusual and would not last, formed a cooperative with branches throughout the territory which would sell and invest the profit as a group. The co-op would also introduce to the planters advanced ideas on crop insurance, spraying and so on, and would cut costs by transporting in bulk — that is, in the co-op trucks. Surplus profit built the headquarters which housed offices and shops. Mr. Bennett, known as "Coffee Bennett," an English planter who had lived there for years and who had their confidence, was the main organizer. The chiefs were put on the executive board, and some of their children were sent abroad to learn cooperative and business administration.

The large building was their pride, and at its opening in the centre of Moshi, Marealle and his retinue which included myself, Coffee Bennett, the District Commissioner and his advisers, all sat at the head table.

Among the crowd, not at the head table, I noticed Julius Nyerere, sitting quite alone. I whispered to Marealle — "Look at Julius, why not invite him to your table?" He grumbled something about his being a troublemaker and dismissed the subject. To be fully understood, this has to be taken in the context of the African social custom — "He with whom the chief smiles is within the blessed power circle." I slipped away and joined Julius.

I asked him how things were going with TANU. He said that the party was increasing but "We have our problems — I'm looking at one of them now," and he was looking in Marealle's direction. They never quarreled, but Marealle did not give him any support.

I tried to form a bridge; they were after all both my friends. I had lived close to Tom and liked him, but I knew that Julius was building a structure for the future, one that was not based on subservience to the British. I asked Nyerere if it wasn't possible to convince Tom that the success of the party was inevitable, a real political force for nation building in which he would have a place as a traditional chief. Nyerere shook his head.

"Julius," I said to him later, "perhaps one of the reasons TANU is not as popular as it could be is that it lacks fire."

"What do you mean?" he asked.

"It's not enough to galvanize a contented people. To fight a cause, you have to fight an enemy. Don't go along with the British system, the British benevolence." As I spoke, I realised he was deep in thought, that he had already come to this realization himself. He later recalled this conversation when in 1971 he paid an official visit to Jamaica as President of Tanzania and where he addressed a joint sitting of both houses of Parliament. I experienced, as a sitting member of that parliament, a moment of special pride to have witnessed the event.

The traumatic events that had begun to take over in Kenya had little effect on the people in Tanganyika, though they did not escape Nyerere. Nyerere and I had one fundamental disagreement. He had asked me to prepare for him a formal argument on my preference for a multi-party system of government. He advocated a single party state. Trained as I was in the Westminster model, where I had gone through the "ABCs" of the colonial system, I emphasized the danger of a dictatorship under one party. "Dudley, you have written a very learned paper — it is most persuasive and worthy of an Oxford graduate. I regret," he went on in a most affable manner, "that I cannot accept your suggestion. It would fractionalize my country, already badly divided. In fact, it is too foreign to us and wouldn't work here." His arguments convinced me as far as Tanganyika was concerned. He added, however, that he believed completely in the necessity to preserve the right to criticize: "We will somehow have to adopt your principle and work it in at every stage of decision-making." I knew he was being kind and attributing to me his own idea. That was Julius — always generous, magnanimous to opposition; it has always been one of his outstanding characteristics.

I will never forget my first meeting with Nyerere, and the great honour of being able to participate in the early struggles of his party. He went on to spread his movement, and I was able to help him internationalize it by writing to those friends I had made in student years. I have watched Nyerere closely over the years. As a political philosopher he is unique, truly an original thinker. As an orator his logic and lucidity have never required the emotional fervor of the demagogue. He was and has always remained the people's champion, and they have given him their undiluted love. Nyerere is a model of the incorruptible ruler who has never been despoiled by his power. His words, though not always supported by the great powers, have always been respected by them. He remains, in the eyes of many, the uncrowned champion of Third World causes.

6 Kenya

Who or what was "Mau Mau?"

While Tanganyika moved peacefully towards independence, the situation in Kenya grew worse. Not for the first time, patriotism was equated with terrorism, and everything that was exclusively African — including the Kikuyu Independent Schools — was looked upon by the government as subversive. In 1949, rumours began spreading about a Kikuyu secret society called "Mau Mau," a society that advocated violence against Europeans. There was talk of strange oath-taking ceremonies and of servants who worked in European homes being lured away or forced to take part in peculiar, mysterious rites. There were also the raids on European farms which left behind mutilated cattle, burning huts and grass fires.

The word "Mau Mau" is not known in any African language. There have been many theories about its origin. One is that it originated among Kikuyu children, as a sort of pass-word used only among themselves while playing. At the approach of a parent or elder, the child who was "look-out" would shout the warning words "mau mau" to the others. "Mau Mau" might have been an inversion of the word "uma uma" or "get away quickly." It was Europeans who first started using the word in a political sense, and it was European response to Mau Mau, in an already tense political atmosphere, that probably made it what it became.

The Kenyan authorities decided that Jomo Kenyatta was becoming too powerful. His oratory was unrivaled, and a message of protest in muted form had started to spread. There is no doubt that the seed of unrest — which erupted into Mau Mau — was arising and spreading out of the KAU meetings. But Kenyatta never advocated subversion or violence. His was a modest request for social, economic and political improvements long overdue. Nevertheless, his meetings were always attended by political informers who made notes and took back reports. The government, which had declared Mau Mau an illegal society, considered Kenyatta the chief instigator of the violence which was slowly taking over in Kenya, and suspected him of being the real leader of the Mau Mau.

The authorities did everything possible to curtail his political activities. I remember often accompanying Kenyatta to the various district commissioners to request permission to hold meetings lawfully. Often we were kept unnecessarily waiting for hours, then ushered into the presence of a young European junior official who would remain seated and interrogate Jomo at length while we stood behind the desk like children before a school master.

Jomo was required to tell him the purpose of the meeting, the names of the speakers, the content of the speeches, the place, time, etc. I always felt degraded and humiliated to see Kenyatta, a leader in his own right and in his own land, treated in this way; and it was always made clear to us that the young European official had complete power to refuse him permission. It became an almost traumatic experience for me to pass from the peaceful happiness of Moshi to the tense war atmosphere of Kenya. Europeans in Kenya looked upon me as some sort of pariah, a traitor to their cause, "on the wrong side," a "communist," and a "disgrace to Oxford." Many were genuinely afraid of Kenyatta because of the propaganda being built around him. Yet Kenyatta more than once, publicly denounced Mau Mau.

At a meeting at Kiambu in August, 1952, tens of thousands flocked to hear him speak. "Sickness of the soul," he said, "cannot be cured by the knife, but by debate; discussion brings agreement, but silence brings hatred and suspicion. If we are to live here in peace and happiness, racial discrimination must be abolished. Our children require good education. We do not want them to be fools. We want higher education subsidised by the government. We pay taxes to help our children. Workers should have their organizations just as in other countries of the world. Successful farmers should be given loans by the government so they can buy machinery and improve their farming in the same way as Europeans. KAU has requested the government to allow Africans to convene meetings and to make their demands known peacefully. If this is agreed, there will be no trouble in this country." He went on to describe Mau Mau as a disease which had to be cured: "Mau Mau has spoiled this country; it must be buried."

All the leading African figures were present at this meeting, including Koinange, Eliud, Mathu and Warihiu. Warihiu was a senior chief, a tall African elegantly dressed in European clothes. He was the government's man, the African who represented colonial policy. He also spoke at this meeting; "Kikuyu land is like the grass blowing one way and another in the breeze of Mau Mau. We have come here to denounce this movement. It has spoiled our country and we do not want it."

It was at this same meeting that old Koinange gave his bitter speech about land ownership. He singled a European out of the crowd and said, "I remember when the first European came to this land. I worked alongside your father, and you are my son."

This was the last time these three, Koinange, Kenyatta and Warihiu, would be seen together publicly.

On October 7, 1952 Warihiu was murdered. The respect of Africans for their chiefs is so deeply embedded that this murder signified something of great local, if not national, importance. And in this case, the killing revealed all the signs of a planned conspiracy.

Travelling in his car from a district he had been visiting, he noticed another car following him. When he ordered his driver to go faster, a chase began. Warihiu managed to reach his destination and stayed there overnight. The next day, he was again followed out on the narrow country road. Reaching a cross-roads the car following his broke away, only to meet him further ahead and block his path. As Warihiu's car drew up, a young Kikuyu leapt from the car, approached Warihiu sitting in the rear, drew a pistol and at point blank range, shot the chief in the chest. He also shot the tires, ran back to the car and drove away. Warihiu's driver had by then fled from the scene.

Koinange was considered the leading suspect — not because any evidence whatsoever tied him to the murder but because, as the most respected and beloved leader of his people, the government, wanting to make an example of someone, chose him. Such was the nation-wide respect for him, that news about his arrest was suppressed. For two days he was transferred from one prison to the next. Fortunately, few secrets remain hidden in Africa. His imprisonment lit a flame in the hearts of the Kikuyu, and word of his arrest travelled quickly to me across the border in neighbouring Tanganyika through their underground, with the speed and in the manner of a forest fire.

No one in the attorney general's office in Nairobi would tell me where Koinange was being held or what charges had been brought against him. I was merely told that he was being detained for questioning. I had a long talk with the attorney general himself and pointed out the precarious situation in Kenya. I said we were sitting on a keg of dynamite that could blow the country sky high, and that all I wanted to do was to represent my client in accordance with British and Kenyan law. This was not the time to deny an old, respected Kikuyu chief his rights. He said he simply could not divulge any information about Koinange, because something very important was about to take place in Kenya. He asked for my co-operation and patience. I could not collaborate in the dark, I replied, adding that if I did not get his support I would apply by "habeas corpus" writ in order to release Koinange. He immediately aborted this by charging Koinange with the murder of Warihiu. This was solely a legal device to prevent him from obtaining bail.

Leaving the attorney general I went from place to place in Nairobi, spending the night with some Indian friends while searching among the Kikuyu for information of Koinange's whereabouts. I was finally told the name of a police station where he was to be taken the following night. I left the same evening. It was quite some distance away and I hoped to reach it in the early hours of the next day before he was moved again.

At the station there was a young, white South African police officer sitting at a desk. I said, "Good morning." He did not bother to reply or look up from his newspaper.

After about a minute, he said, "Yes?"

"I'm here to represent Chief Koinange."

He looked up, very startled, first because no one was supposed to know that Koinange was there, and second, because he had probably never before been spoken to in that manner by a Black man.

"Who told you he was here? What authority do you have to come here?"

"It's no concern of yours, but I found out he is here — and he is here. The only authority I need is here with me." I showed him that I was qualified in the United Kingdom as a barrister-at-law and accepted by the bars of Kenya and Tanganyika.

"My instructions are to allow no one to see him. In fact, I'm not even admitting that he is here." He sat back in his chair, smiling.

"Kindly let me use that telephone," and before he could say "no," I picked up the phone and called the attorney general.

Reaching him I said: "I am at ——— station to see my client and there is a police officer here who is being rude and intransigent. Please advise him that if he doesn't co-operate I will hold him responsible for holding a prisoner without due authority."

He asked me to hand the phone over to the officer and I don't know what passed between them, but the officer respectfully repeated "Yes, Sir," several times, and put back the phone. There was a miraculous change in his attitude. He shouted to one of the African guards nearby and said: "Bring Koinange."

I said: "No, I would like to be taken to him. Under the law I am entitled to see the condition in which he is kept."

The African guard had been watching the whole scene with frightened excitement, certain that a Black man could not get away with speaking to a white officer as I had. The officer, realizing he was being watched, could not let me win the whole show. "Bring Koinange," he repeated in an angry shout.

I will never forget the rest.

The old man, bent with age and the indignities heaped upon him, came out of his dark cell, his eyes squinting to adjust to ordinary daylight. This man who had always been impeccably dressed was now barefoot, wearing nothing above the waist, and holding up a pair of baggy prison trousers much too large for his shrivelled body. Seeing me he was so overcome that he let them fall to the ground as he hugged me, naked as a baby.

"Thank God you have come for me, Dudley. What is happening to me? What is happening in this country? I hear strange things. They move me like a thief in the night from station to station. Where are my wives? What is happening to my home? I beg you to take me home."

He was sobbing against my chest like a child, all his words in Swahili, spilling out at once. I later heard that in each of the stations to which he had been taken, so respected was this man among Africans that the African prisoners stripped themselves of their clothes at night in order to make bedding for their chief. As he stood there naked and crying I swore I would not leave Kenya before this battle was over. I was going to fight for this man's rights and fight to end the oppressive system that could reduce this great man, the father of Africa, to a dribbling, demoralized creature shut away in a dark cell.

I visited him often in the Nairobi prison where he was later kept. I saw how the racial and social divisions were maintained even in the prisons, and often the picture of blindfolded justice came to me. Most of the prisoners were Africans — sentenced for not paying hut taxes or some such infringement. They slept many to a cell and wore short prison trousers and canvas shirts. There were a sprinkling of Indians, usually there for fraud, embezzlement or similar offences. They wore long trousers and slept on mattresses, not the cold cement floor as did the Africans. A rarity was a European in prison. I saw one, in for murdering his wife. He not only wore his own clothes, but slept on a bed and had his laundry done by African prisoners. Thus even in prison this uneven and unholy Trinity was evident. But the Kikuyu continued to strip themselves to provide bed and blankets for Koinange.

separation even in prison!

It was many weeks before Koinange was brought to trial. The police tried all the means at their disposal, including bribery and torture, to make out a case of murder against him. As counsel for the accused I continuously complained about the signs of beating and physical mistreatment of the various co-accused and even witnesses. These complaints all fell on deaf ears. Eventually the crown, feeling they had a good case against my client (there was even talk of a confession), held the preliminary investigation, and in the expected atmosphere of hostility, Koinange and others were committed for trial. The charge was conspiracy to murder.

I wrote to Sir Dingle Foot in London — under whose tutelage I had served as a barrister after leaving Oxford — and he came out to Kenya to lead me in the defence of Koinange.

During this time of waiting for Koinange's case to be brought to trial, events had escalated in Kenya — Jomo Kenyatta had been detained.

7 State of Emergency

A state of emergency was declared on October 20, 1952 — not long after the arrest of Koinange. The Kikuyu Independent Schools were closed down and all public meetings banned. The police immediately put into effect "Operation Jock Scoot," a military-police operation, in order to completely crush the nationalist movement. Nairobi took on the appearance of disorderly preparation for war. There was an unusually great number of askaris and white officers in the streets. Roadblocks sprang up at provincial crossroads. Police stations and government buildings were sandbagged and strategic areas encircled by barbed wire. Groups of Africans, mainly Kikuyu, were seen herded — hands placed uncomfortably on their heads — along the streets into the barbed wire enclosures. Under the emergency measures, any Kikuyu could be detained and questioned in connection with Mau Mau.

Previously I had contacted many leaders of the banned Kenya African Union, in particular Kenyatta, whom I had warned to secure legal assistance in advance. He saw and understood what the many sudden police searches were leading to, and without the slightest show of fear, said "Yes, Dudley. You and I must make plans." We approached many lawyers. No European in Kenya would touch any case involving him, and the Indian lawyers offered no more than pleasant excuses and an occasional cup of tea. Again I wrote to friends in England and the West Indies, progressive liberals, informing them of the state of affairs in Kenya. I also advised Mbiu Koinange, son of the old Chief, to remain in London where he was studying. Leaders of KAU also took my advice, raised funds and spirited Fred Murumbi out of Kenya. Murumbi was an African of Masai ancestry who would later become Kenya's first Minister of Foreign Affairs. Expecting that any day Kenyatta and the others might be detained, we made arrangements for KAU to carry on meetings in Uganda and Tanganyika. I recall going with Kenyatta to several lawyers for assistance in vain. There was always an excuse as to why they could not help.

Koinange's trial overlapped the strange events surrounding Kenyatta's detention, and I found myself at times travelling hundreds of miles each day between the two cases.

The trial of Chief Koinange was something of a "cause celebre" and the pomp and ceremony of the administration of British justice lost none of its colour in Nairobi's supreme court. The huge impressive building which housed the several courts was majestic with its tall columns and graceful arches. The law library was up-to-date and well-stocked with legal books; the rooms and chambers spacious and comfortable with large ceiling fans. The crimson-robed judges, whose white wigs of artificial curls fell to their shoulders, were of course, all English. All of the lawyers in and out of the court were English or Indian, and wore flowing black gowns, starched white collars and shorter white wigs. The proceedings were strictly British throughout and utterly polite.

For some strange reason the rules of evidence followed the Indian code, but everything else was a direct copy of the United Kingdom. Juries were only used in European cases, i.e. when Europeans were being tried, and then the jury was completely European. Africans were tried by a judge, who had two local assessors to advise him on local law or custom. He was of course not bound by their opinion. There was usually one interpreter to interpret any other indigenous language into Swahili, and another to interpret from Swahili into English.

Outside the court on the neatly-kept lawns were groups of Africans who were allowed to sit on the grass. One can only imagine what thoughts they entertained as they witnessed the foreign procedures carried on in a strange tongue. Somehow they got the message that I was on their side, and they showed great deference to me when I drove up in the mornings. They offered to carry my bags, my books, to stay by my car, and welcomed me with smiles of hope and looks of recognition. To them, I represented one from abroad, distantly related by colour though not of their tribe, one who understood the legal "magic," and was in some way their protector. Each day they came in increasing numbers, and a few were allowed into the public gallery. Those few who followed the interpreters inside brought out their own versions to their friends outside at the end of the day.

I acted as junior counsel to Dingle Foot. I learned much from him in the practice at the bar. The case against Koinange as presented by the crown sought to associate him, as the spiritual leader and most beloved head of the Kikuyu tribe, as part of the Mau Mau conspiracy to carry out the murder of Warihiu. One little known story of the trial was an offer of clemency to one of the accused — Warihiu's driver — if he would sign a confession implicating Koinange. The driver bravely said he would rather face the gallows than tell a lie against his chief.

The announcement of the state of emergency had sent tremors all around. Before the shock was properly felt, severe and restrictive regulations were passed such as the *kipande* or pass laws. This forbade Africans not living in their own areas to go without passes. They could be stopped and searched at will, and they were. Trucks, buses and cars were searched and the jails began to overflow. Camps with barbed wire fences and guard towers with search lights and armed police were erected to receive the steady flow of African men, women and children — all detained at "Her Majesty's pleasure." Many just went "missing." People were stopped and taken out of their vehicles on city streets and herded into captivity. Families were separated. A large African market, known as Burma Market, the largest in Nairobi, was set on fire. It burned for days. At one point, the government brought some policemen from a different area into Nairobi and they immediately went berserk, beating, gun-butting and generally terrorizing the Kikuyu. The Kikuyu were the main target of the Kenyan authorities in their effort to eradicate the Mau Mau. And Mau Mau continued, shadowy, invisible, like the slow turning of the worm in the earth, turning in every direction, impossible to dismember. I would hear constantly of a raid on an outlying farm which had left some cattle mutilated, or of a hut set on fire or some workman chopped to death by *pangas* — short sharp instruments which were the agricultural tool of most African farm-workers. Most of the Africans killed this way were "loyalists," that is, those who collaborated with the Europeans. Interestingly, not a single European was attacked until after the arrests of Kenyatta and the other KAU leaders.

It got to be a common sight — police or soldiers marching Kikuyu men and women into hastily erected barbed-wire stockades. Hundreds of these prisons sprang up. Sometimes trucks and buses carrying workmen or women to the markets or to farms were stopped, searched, and either all or some were taken off and sent into these camps, not to be heard about sometimes for days after diligent searching by relatives or employers. If the employer was European and could vouch for their innocence, many could be released. But most did not have this backing. They suffered in silence, herded together in the dark steaming overcrowded prisons. Especially as the police paid for information, it turned out to be a happy hunting season for those settling old scores or jealousies, or just keeping in good grace with the authorities.

Many Africans, to protect themselves, pointed a finger, true or false, and elected to play the role of informer rather than be arrested. The period was really one of utmost confusion. The interrogations carried out night and day by the police were atrocious, even bestial. Some are too obscene or gruesome to be described here. I recall several times during the emergency lodging complaints about ill treatment. They all fell on deaf ears.

One morning on my way to meet a British cabinet minister, Mr. Arthur Bottomly, who was heading a parliamentary mission to a Commonwealth meeting in Nairobi, I saw something that completely outraged me. I passed some forty or fifty Africans squatting on their heels in the road with their hands clasped over their heads. Unfortunately, this was not unusual. But squatting painfully amongst the crowd in the main street of Nairobi, was my good friend Tom Mboya — handsomely dressed in a pin-striped tailored suit. He had been pulled out of his car on his way to work. Secretary General of the African Trade Union and a graduate of Oxford, had he lived, I am sure Mboya would have succeeded Kenyatta as president of Kenya. I came out of my car and pointed to him as I approached a young officer, flanked by askari.

"Do you know who this is?" I shouted. "He is Tom Mboya."

"Get the hell out of here," he replied.

In a rage, I moved out of the grasp of the askari who had come towards me, and went to my car. I drove quickly to the New Stanley Hotel and there confronted the colonial secretary, James Griffiths, and Arthur Bottomly, both of whom were genuinely ashamed and promised to make representations at the conference which was about to take place. This was just one of the many daily incidents that drove me to the brink of frustration. Mboya would later be featured on the cover of *Time* magazine as minister of state and praised for his eloquence and leadership abilities.

On one of my visits across the border of Kenya I visited some elders who consulted me on the government's destruction of the Kikuyu Independent Schools. The police and military, in joint operations, were either burning the schools' buildings or converting them with barbed wire into detention camps for the Kikuyu. These schools had been the hope and pride of their districts. The villagers had volunteered their labour and material to erect the thatched buildings. Now the parents took their children to watch, observe and remember what the white imperialists were doing to them. They watched in silence, little groups of families holding hands some distance away among the sheltering trees, as they saw their beloved schools razed to the ground. There was no mistaking the pain and anguish in the minds of these helpless families. It added one more reason for hatred as the flames went up. They stood as at a funeral pyre; mothers, fathers and children, until only ashes remained, then they disappeared silently into the forests hoping to see their own homes safe on their return. This, like the village arrests, only hardened the spirit of resistance. It was on visits like these that I learned what was going on in the country. I knew I was being watched. I had complete freedom of movement — no doubt for good reasons. I rarely slept at the same house twice. Africans with whom I lodged would often be detained the following day. I began to stay at the homes of Indian friends who were sympathetic to the African cause.

Chief Koinange's trial had been slowly dragging behind the tedious procedures of the high court in Nairobi. Dingle Foot and myself went through a maze of evidence, none of which was even slightly incriminating of Koinange. He was proven innocent and acquitted — to loud rejoicing from the crowd who had patiently followed the trial day after day. I even saw several Europeans weeping openly with joy at his acquittal, so clear was his innocence and the complete unfairness of his arrest all along. But the rejoicing was short-lived, almost momentary. On the release of this aged, respectable man, nearly a century old, he was immediately detained outside the court house and taken away under the new emergency orders.

Koinange was eventually released only a short time before he died. He was taken to his ancestral home of Kiambu where I had enjoyed many happy days with him and his family. Here I had felt the pulse of the Kikuyu and had entered within the very heart of the people. To listen to the old man was to relive the history of East Africa before the English introduced the cruel aspects of their colonizing with all its plunders and injustices. They had robbed a contented people of their ancient dignity and peaceful way of life.

Years later after Kenya had won her independence, I visited the country again as Jamaica's foreign minister with a delegation of five. I had especially asked to visit Koinange's grave and was taken there by Mbiu Koinange, son of the old Chief and now a Minister of State. On the way to Kiambu the car stopped. Our escort left the car and went out to speak to one of the Kikuyu women who had been passing the roadside with a load of firewood on her head. They spoke together in Kikuyu and she turned to look at us. Suddenly she dropped her load and dashed over to us, threw her arms inside the window and hugged me effusively. She was one of Koinange's daughters. We went with her to Kiambu and on the way she told me all the news of the intervening years, about the old man's death and how he had said as he way dying that one day I would return. She presented me with a very old ivory walking stick inlaid with ebony, which Koinange had left for me. It is still one of my prized possessions.

It became quite clear to me that the Kenya government was responding to the overt pressure of the white minority to stamp out Mau Mau, regarded by them as a satanic secret society both barbarous and subversive. Their difficulty lay in the character of the Kikuyu who skillfully refused, even under severe torture, to reveal either membership in, or knowledge of Mau Mau. The government's approach was hardly likely to bear fruit, and certainly could not bring co-operation. In the place of scientific investigation, they depended on high-handed brutality, and assumed that if you were Kikuyu, you were at least guilty of complicity in this evil thing. The Kikuyu suffered much, but silently. Their lips were sealed. The oaths held them, and they were loyal to their leaders. Those who assisted the police often came to a brutal end. I sensed that ahead of us lay a horrifying bloodbath (unless leaders on both sides, white and Black, could come together and make concessions).

In the period just before the State of Emergency, I had made an appointment with the commissioner of police. He was a giant of a man and had once been a member of the Canadian Mounted Police. He received me very pleasantly, no doubt enjoying the novelty of talking with a Black man who was not afraid of him. Outside his office Masai occasionally walked by, some of them six and a half feet or more, daubed with red paint and with ever present spear held lightly in one hand.

My request to Mr. Timmerman was that a group of us should meet in order to find ways to head off an uprising. I undertook to bring to my side of the table, Jomo Kenyatta and six or more leading Africans whom Mr. Timmerman could name. I requested that the attorney general along with himself appear on the other side with whomever they cared to invite. We spoke for nearly an hour without moving a single inch towards agreement. His assistants occasionally looked in and showed their surprise at seeing us in such close and serious conversation. One of them came in and stayed for a while — I remember clearly — Inspector Heine. He was particularly evil and was later dismissed in disgrace from the service. Timmerman's final answer was blunt: "We are not gong to sit and talk with murderers, cattle thieves and barbarians. We are going to teach them a lesson that they will never forget in this country."

I remember answering him with some sadness, "History will note that you had an alternative at half-past eleven before the midnight into which you are about to plunge."

"To teach a lesson," said Mr. Timmerman, and subsequently several thousand lives were lost and at least 50,000 detained. The intransigence on the part of the whites in Kenya was stupefying, as it is today in South Africa. If there were a lesson to be learned by the bloodshed and atrocities which followed, it is that Africans would no longer be bullied and harassed in their own country, that — in the later words of a British prime minister — "the winds of change" were already sweeping across Africa.

During that tense and difficult time in Kenya, I still managed to keep my practice as a lawyer going in Tanganyika. One day while at court in Moshi, I received an unusual phone call from Arusha. Arusha, the provincial capital, is some fifty-five miles to the north of Moshi almost on the border with Kenya. The magistrate asked me to take the call in the privacy of his office and he left the room. It was a call from the provincial commissioner himself, a very senior officer, subordinate only to the governor. He said that although we had never met, he was well acquainted with my work as a lawyer and there was something he wanted to discuss with me rather urgently, something that he couldn't discuss on the telephone. I consulted my diary and suggested some dates within a fortnight. His reply was that it was a matter of such national importance that he would give me his assurance that the courts would do everything to facilitate me, by postponing at my convenience other unfinished matters, and added that this request had come from the highest quarters.

Sensing that it was something out of the ordinary I promised to come the next day.

Arusha is a very clean modern town in the heart of Africa. It is about as far from Cairo as it is from Cape Town. It lies on the southern slope of Mount Arusha and one can view from certain points at the same time both Mount Kenya and Kilimanjaro. It had an unusually large white population. Most of the homes were neat little red brick bungalows with flower gardens surrounded by picket fences — a picture of English suburbia. It was also the centre of the safari hunting trade. Tours originated there and many a white hunter could be distinguished by his dress on the stools of the European bars or the verandahs of the houses: safari jacket, short trousers, floppy hat, distinctly East African. They wouldn't live anywhere else. They made a rough but handsome living as guides, assisting in the shooting of wild game, with tourists and the film companies. Driving along the Sterling-Astaldi highway from Moshi to Arusha I had passed herds of zebra and elephants, the graceful swift gazelles, the ever-present ostriches, giraffes and monkeys, the latter swinging from limb to limb in the trees; and dotting the hillsides were the Masai, tending herds of cows, standing elegantly at rest on one leg and leaning against their slender spears.

The provincial commissioner's office was very easy to find. Painted a glittering official white with a Union Jack flying before it, it stood on very spacious grounds where many a garden party must have feted officials on holiday. A British soldier led me into the highly polished office, smartly saluted the commissioner and withdrew. The commissioner put me very much at ease in a spacious leather chair and offered me a cigar and some tea. I refused both, politely, as he kept up with his small talk. Dressed in white, he was a big man in every sense, frank and friendly in his approach — a professional colonial official.

He spoke of the tragedies in Kenya, the "Mau Mau menace," the deaths and destruction and the reminder that Arusha was the province nearest Kenya. He added that information had come to him that Kenyans in Tanganyika would soon spread the conflagration to our territory and that this had to be stopped at all costs and quickly. I listened in silence, although there were many significant pauses on his part. These were clearly invitations for me to comment. He continued: "In fact, it has already begun."

He sat forward upon saying this and looked me squarely in the eyes as I raised a quizzical eyebrow. This was news to me. I wondered if he was going to refer to the many visits I made through Arusha en route to Kenya, and if the many visitors who had come to me under the cover of night from various parts of Kenya had at last been observed.

"It is believed," he went on, "that you can be of great service to us, and I have been asked by the highest officials here and in Kenya to approach you."

This greatly increased my curiosity, not only the joint interest of both countries, but because I knew that the only officials higher than himself were the governors of both countries.

"Let me put it squarely on the table," he said. "Several of our most influential farmers in this province have complained that their Kikuyu workers have been molested — in fact tortured. This, they claim, has been done to them by Kenya police officers and their aides — illegally — in this territory. They are hunting down Kikuyu who they claim are members of the Mau Mau. The farmers say it is wreaking havoc among the workers of their farms, and they want immediate action taken against these illegal intrusions. I have had to lay serious charges of aggravated assault against a European named Brian Hayworth and about thirty Africans who have collaborated with him in inflicting punishment on the Kikuyu. Will you take the case for their defence?"

It is an understatement to say that this took me by surprise.

I needed some time to consider this. The governments of both Kenya and Tanganyika were asking me to defend men who had tortured Kikuyu farm workers! The question had been straightforwardly put and I told him I needed time and to hear more facts before replying. He invited me to dine and handed me a bulky file, then asked a very attractive, prim and proper looking English secretary to make an office next door available to me. I spent over two hours examining the brief. It came as no surprise to me that the signed complaints were made almost exclusively by continental Europeans — Danes, Greeks and some Germans of Tanganyika, as opposed to the English and South African farmers of Kenya. It had long been my observation that in matters of race relations the Africans received far better treatment from the continental Europeans than from the English, Rhodesians and Afrikaners.

These briefs read like the worst horror stories of fiction. Though they were summaries, they outlined the torture of scores of Kikuyu farm workers by African aides under the direct orders of Captain Hayworth. It was no surprise to me that whereas the aides were held in the Arusha prison, Hayworth was out on bail, under house arrest in a comfortable hotel in Arusha.

Later, over a typically English meal of lamb with mint sauce, excellently served by Kenyan servants in starched uniforms and white gloves (stamped "Elizabeth R" in scarlet red), we discussed the matter further. I told him that my role in East Africa had always been clearly identified with Africans and in particular with the Kikuyu cause. I had to consider the question of the future confidence of my clientele if I accepted this case. His reply was clear and instantaneous: "Be assured the matter has not escaped us. If you find it impossible to accept, my superiors will understand. They have given me a free hand to discuss it with you, and I must tell you that your reputation at the bar is known in both areas and I hope you will somehow find it possible to accept." I felt, and still feel, that he was an honest man handling a difficult situation. After a short silence I accepted, on condition that I defended the Africans only, and that other arrangements be made for Hayworth, and also that I had freedom to carry out my duties without any government interference. I added that I would interrogate my clients individually and alone. The conditions were accepted and I agreed to take the brief for the defence of the Africans charged.

I took this case mainly hoping to expose to the people of Tanganyika and elsewhere the kind of atrocities being carried out with the approval of the Kenyan government. I made several visits to my clients, the African police aides, in their prison in Arusha. They were unusually confident, almost cocky in their self-assurance. They were tough, trained sadists from Kenya who had been successfully beating up their fellow men. They were a junior branch — though only semi-officially — of the Kenya Police Force. In these men there was neither fear of punishment nor any moral element of contrition. In fact, they were dehumanized and well on their way to becoming utter morons of a particularly nasty and brutal type. They spoke to me with unabashed truthfulness and I took down their every word. Those who could write, one out of five, signed their names, and all affixed their fingerprints to their individual statements. It would be nauseating to repeat them here and I shall try to typify them in general remarks.

They had been brought in trucks to Tanganyika by Captain Hayworth, across a border which meant nothing to them. The farms around Arusha, though a few miles apart, were not far from their own neighbourhood in Kenya. Their routine was to visit a European farm which had previously been visited by Hayworth, in groups or alone, as if looking for employment on the farm. They would mingle easily with the workmen and in a short time could distinguish the Kikuyu from the other Africans. When Captain Hayworth returned, the Kikuyu were separated from the others and taken either to a farm sympathetic to Kenya's policies or to some distant huts on the same farm. They were all asked to sign a paper confessing to being members of the Mau Mau. They did not know, many of them, that this was a crime punishable in itself. Displayed very prominently on the table where they signed, was a *kiboko* or rhinoceros hide whip, a South African specialty, guaranteed to lacerate the toughest skin. The Kenyan aides were all expert in its handling and could flick it accurately so as to make it crack like a rifle shot. This they did frequently, just to begin the terror. Those who signed were immediately taken away. The others were questioned.

The first few questions were given within the hearing of all: "Who is the Mau Mau treasurer on this farm?" or "Who visited you from Nairobi?" or "Which of these others is a member of the Mau Mau?" The answers were written down, or a pretence was made of doing so. The questions were loud, rough and threatening. Some were then removed from sight, but not out of hearing, and the torture began. They could hear the lashes and the loud bawling of the tortured, the crying. The bleeding body, often only partly conscious and moaning was always carried past those awaiting their turn. In most cases Hayworth himself administered the flogging until he was tired then passed the job to one of his aides who was waiting or holding down the unfortunate man. There were other treatments such as hanging them by a rope from their wrists as they were beaten, so that they barely touched the ground with their toes. The blood was alternately washed off with hot and cold water. One old man had a very large stone placed on his chest and died from broken ribs and internal bleeding. Some were beaten on the soles of their feet till they could not stand. One poor soul, immediately after the torture, stole away in the night from his hospital bed and hanged himself from a tree. This was his escape.

The trial itself, which took place several weeks later, was one of the most unusual affairs I have ever participated in professionally. There had been no collaboration whatsoever between Hayworth's defence lawyer, the attorney general's office and myself. We met for the first time in the court at Arusha where I understood right away that some "arrangements" had been made with the judge. I gathered that what the American judicial system calls "plea bargaining" had taken place. This has no recognition in Kenyan law. The party charged pleads guilty and the judge is spared the trouble of going into the evidence and a full trial, and as a result compensates by giving a very lenient sentence. That is plea bargaining, which I repeat has no place in our jurisprudence. I further realized that it had been agreed that on a plea of guilty the lightest sentence would be imposed and no details given in evidence. In short, the trial was going to be nothing but a formal procedure to whitewash the cruelties and hide the gory details.

I kept my peace. Hayworth, being European, was called first. he pleaded guilty and stood down in the well of the court with his family and friends to await sentencing later.

They brought up the aides, five at a time as the dock was not large enough to hold them all. The first pleaded "not guilty." The court fell silent. The judge said: "Stand down, bring me the next." The second did the same. After each plea the judge is supposed to write in his book, which is the official record of the court. It became clear after the fourth or so that my instructions called for a full trial for my clients on such a plea. The judge interrupted the proceedings and asked me whether I was not doing my clients more harm than good, intimating that if he had to try them on the full exposition of the grisly facts, they would no doubt get a much stiffer sentence. I insisted that the law follow its normal course and that I was pleading "respondent superior," that is — that they acted under orders. The judge decided to take over from me and asked each of my clients — "Did you beat so and so?" On their reply, "Yes, I did," he announced that he was changing their pleas to one of "guilty," thus bypassing the necessity to give evidence and thereby not revealing to the press and to the public the facts of the dastardly tortures. He was quite wrong in law, of course, not to accept their plea of "not guilty." He then called them all up before him. He fined Hayworth a few shillings which his family promptly paid, and sentenced the Africans to a short jail term which included the time they had already spent, and in fact was so short that they would be free on the rising of the court. Further, I had no right to appeal, as their plea of guilty had been entered in the judge's record, nor could I argue the sentencing. The matter was closed. Hayworth returned to Kenya, warned by the authorities not to return to Tanganyika, and the latter were satisfied with the appearance that justice had been done.

Under the guise of suppressing an African secret society called Mau Mau, the British in Kenya were fighting a people's liberation movement. It did not start as such and was difficult to be observed as such at the beginning because the sides were so unevenly matched. The Africans were unarmed except for their ancient spears and *pangas*. The British, in addition to the King's African Rifles and the armed police, sent out a squadron of the Royal Air Force to hunt and pursue the Kikuyu, many of whom had taken to the mountains which they knew well. Many new laws and regulations were passed against them. Eventually there were some eighteen or nineteen offences all punishable by death or long sentences of many years including "being found in possession of anything capable of starting a fire." Indeed I had over and over again to argue that this went even further than possessing a box of matches since Africans often cooked their food by rubbing two sticks together; but the "justice" of the Kenya courts went on relentlessly.

8 Kapenguria

Shortly, in fact an hour after the state of emergency had been declared, Jomo Kenyatta and five other KAU leaders were detained. As I described at the opening of this book, Kenyatta was awakened at night by six African soldiers pointing rifles at him while a white officer explained that he was being detained under the emergency laws. He was allowed to take a small suitcase of clothes, but not told where he was being taken, or what charges where being brought against him. Before leaving the house he asked for some writing paper and was handed an envelope. On this he wrote my name and address and gave it to the officer in charge, saying, "Please send to Moshi for my lawyer, Dudley Thompson."

He was taken to a military airfield outside Nairobi and flown to Lokitaung, a small district near the Ethiopian border. There he was joined by five other so-called leaders of the Mau Mau.

I never received that envelope. There is evidence pointing to the possibility that the authorities wanted to quietly "eliminate" Kenyatta and stifle the nationalist cause. Their efforts might have succeeded if not for the courage and initiative of a certain European living in Kenya who brought a message to me.

It was a Saturday afternoon and I was at home cleaning my guns in preparation for hunting, my favourite pastime, in probably the best game area in the world. Here were gazelles, impalas, wild boar, guinea fowl, greater kufu, geese, you name it — a hunter's paradise. There was also the big game: rhinoceros, elephants, lion, leopard, cheetah and dangerous snakes in all the bushes. These were usually reserved for the white hunters, professionals who for a fee took safari parties on hunting expeditions.

My house-servant, Mohammed, came in with a strange air of excitement:

"Bwana, mgeni awaka kuzungumza siri" ("Sir, a stranger wants to talk to you privately").

"Mgeni gani?" ("What kind of stranger?") I asked.

"Mzungu" ("a white man").

I went out to meet him. He was dishevelled and unshaven and had driven for two days and nights, practically without stopping, to deliver a message to me. He refused the offer to wash and shave, but dined with me, and seated at the table immediately blurted out "I've been sent by Mr. Kenyatta to give you a message."

I had never seen this man before and my instincts told me to be cautious. "Where did you see him? How is he? Did he send a note?" I must say, he conveyed an air of urgency and sincerity.

"I left him in the Court House at Kapenguria in North Kenya. They brought him there with the others and released them from detention, but planned to put them on trial there Wednesday. It will take you a few days to get there and he asked me to tell you to hurry. They're kept incommunicado — no letters, or telephones. Because you don't know me he told me to tell you. . . ." And he went on to relate something only Kenyatta and I shared. It went back to our days together in Britain. The stranger stressed that I should let no one know he had brought me this message, that it would be dangerous for him. He is still alive today and I still honour that request for anonymity. He did Kenyatta, and the whole country, an invaluable and unforgettable service.

I immediately began to prepare to go to Kapenguria. He gave me a road map which included, after Nairobi, large areas traversed only by elephant trails and some desert. The journey would be over nine hundred miles. I packed for two weeks and tried in vain to find out the actual charges being laid against Kenyatta. He knew only that it had to do with Mau Mau and that the judge would be the notorious Judge Thacker. Thacker had already retired. He had earned a reputation as the darling of the white plantocracy, and had been sworn in specially for this trial. I later learned that a special queen's counsel had been sent for from the United Kingdom — Mr. Somerhough, Q.C. — to lead the prosecution. I found him to be a very able prosecutor who dealt straight from the top of the deck — an English professional, in clear contrast with the judge who was atrociously biased.

The first thing I did was to go to the district commissioner for a pass for entry into all roads. This district commissioner, a South African Rhodes scholar, had over the years of my dealings with him shown himself to be very fair-minded and helpful. As his jurisdiction only extended as far as Tanganyika, he telephoned his counterpart across the border for a pass for me to enter all roads for an indefinite period. I explained to him that I could not be more specific in my request and he was very kind and obliging in this respect. The pass proved of the greatest assistance later when I had to roam all over the many closed areas of Kenya to collect witnesses and evidence.

I drove without stopping through Arusha, Lai-tok-i-tak, and other towns and settlements, stopping only to refuel, and to fill extra vessels with fuel and water, as there were many miles between petrol stations. I also had my rifle and revolver with me. Mile after mile, I had only my own thoughts for company. There was nothing on the radio about the impending trial. I realized this was only to be the facade of a trial in order to put Kenyatta away along with the other leaders of the movement, a trial for which he had no preparation, no defending lawyer and no chance. The dice were not only loaded against us; there were no dice at all in this game.

The journey after Arusha alternated between long stretches of dusty trail and miles of asphalt highway nearing Nairobi. I collected my pass in Kenya en route. Occasionally I passed a herd of gazelles hopping across the plains. The giraffes looked unreal with their long necks as they delicately nibbled the tender shoots and the tops of trees, then loped awkwardly with deceptive speed upon my approach. I noticed that unlike other animals, when they ran both legs on each side moved together and parallel at the same time. Monkeys chattered in the trees. Large herds of wildebeest — a cousin of the American bison — galloped together. The beautiful, striped zebras completed the scene. Now and then in this wilderness I came upon a Masai, or a Mwarusha man walking miles in a majestic and untiring stride, going, it seemed to me, from nowhere to nowhere. Or groups of three or four Masai women with babies on their backs, elegant and tall, some over six feet, wearing beaten cow-skins as soft as linen, embroidered with coloured beads. Often they carried large gourds on their shaven heads and numerous beaded ornaments around their necks and ankles. On and on the journey continued.

I caught a few hours sleep in Nairobi and posted a few letters to Jamaica and England — to Padmore and others — telling friends where I was going and why. I slept at the house of Josephine Muthoni, an African lady of great beauty, regal in appearance and bearing. She was a Kikuyu business woman who owned a bar and several taxis. She was married to one of Koinange's sons and was the mother of four sons. I became very fond of the family. On my return to Jamaica I sent for her son Lawrence, who was educated in Jamaica, and later at a university in the United States where he graduated. Unfortunately, while attending law school at Howard, he had a tragic car accident and died one week before he was due to return home for a visit to his mother in Africa. The family often practised their English with me. Josephine spoke only Swahili and Kikuyu. She made many sacrifices to the Kikuyu cause and paid dearly for it later — she was taken from her car one day in Nairobi and hustled into detention many miles away.

I managed to reach Kapenguria only a few hours before the "trial" was due to begin. I was dead tired, unshaven and badly in need of a bath. I introduced myself to Somerhough, told him I would be representing Kenyatta but would be applying for an adjournment that day. He suggested that we approach the judge in chambers so as not to take him by surprise. This was good advice. We both asked for an audience and having knocked at his chambers — in the converted schoolhouse surrounded with barbed wire and manned at each corner by Kenya African Rifles, soldiers carrying Vickers machine guns — we were told that the judge was already on his way to the bench and we should make our application in open court. The prisoners had not yet been brought in, and were in fact sent back after my application. I had not seen them. Somerhough raised an eyebrow and shrugged his shoulders as we both returned to our benches in the court. Justice Thacker was making it clear beyond a doubt that this was his court and he was solely in charge. He had been sent there with clear instructions and would brook no interference in carrying them out.

Kapenguria, I must explain, is a name that only became well-known through the notoriety of the trial of Jomo Kenyatta. An outpost of the Suk district, it looks out from its heights on the mountains of Ethiopia. There was no town. The area was very underdeveloped. Many men and women walked around almost completely naked. They carried very slender spears and were reputed, in these colonial times, to be very fierce. Even in normal times, Suk was "closed country," which meant that you needed a special pass to visit the area. Aside from the schoolhouse and what may have been a teacher's cottage vacated for the judge, I only saw a few huts in the entire area. The soldiers had pitched tents and were there in great numbers. Later, during the trial, they would pitch a larger tent, or marquee, for the reporters and European guests who came to attend the trial. Africans were not allowed in the area except for the Suk people, who took no apparent interest but showed their disagreement at being photographed by tourists and newsmen.

On the opening of the court, Mr. Somerhough announced: "My learned friend, Mr. Thompson, wishes, my Lord, to make an application to the court."

I rose, but before I could speak, the judge intervened.

"Mr. Thompson, how do you come to be appearing for these accused?"

I was sure from his tone that he wanted to know by what means I had heard of the trial. I feigned ignorance of this and replied: "Is your Lordship requesting to see my qualifications to appear?"

"Well, I will certainly have to be satisfied with that as well."

I produced the necessary documents which showed my admission to the Kenyan Bar.

"How were you instructed?" he pursued.

I replied that that was privileged information and in any case, irrelevant, and added that I was applying for an adjournment to study the case.

"On what grounds do you base this application? Do you know how much it is costing the government per day to hold this inquiry, and have you any idea how long it will take to go through all that evidence?" Here he pointed to a trestle in the court, laden with books, papers and other documents.

"My Lord," I replied, "I don't know what relevance these questions have to me now. In a case where neither my clients nor myself have been served with either indictment or information, I am completely unable to advise my clients or, indeed, to receive their instructions. As to the documents referred to, no doubt the crown has had time to study them. But we were brought to court without the slightest preparation, and in the interest of justice, I at least require to be served with the charges and to instruct my clients accordingly."

"Mr. Somerhough, have you anything to say relative to this unusual application? I suppose you are ready to proceed."

"I hardly see how I can oppose his application my Lord; indeed I am prepared to commence, but only just, as I have not been long in the colony and could use the time to good advantage myself."

The judge, clearly disappointed, then asked me: "How much time are you asking for?"

"My Lord, it's hard to say since I haven't even seen the charges."

"Pass them to him," he ordered, whereupon a clerk handed me a thick sheaf of papers, almost a pamphlet, containing numerous offences. Without reading them I proposed that the court adjourn for the day to give me time to read through and consult my clients, not yet in the dock.

"Impossible," Thacker shouted. "Court adjourns till 2 p.m., at which time we will continue to hear this application without further delay." And he left the room.

Somerhough put his pipe in his mouth, an inveterate habit, and gave me what I thought was a sympathetic smile. He said nothing and withdrew. I sat down and immediately began to read through the headings as I could not possibly study the whole thing in the time allowed. I left the court and discovered from an African attendant and sweeper that there was only one hotel within five miles but that it was strictly for Europeans only. I would have to take the long journey of three hundred miles to Nairobi twice daily by car.

When we resumed at 2 p.m., I was barely aware of the nature of the charges. They seemed to vary in specifics among the several accused, but some were general like "participation in an illegal association." Kenyatta was charged on many counts, including being leader and manager of the Mau Mau, an outlawed society, and with officiating at certain illegal ceremonies, the administering of ceremonial oaths, etc. It was obvious just from the part I had scanned in the allotted time that it was going to be a long and difficult trial, that much preparation would be required, and that my limited experience was not up to the task. I would need the best defence lawyer available. I applied for an adjournment of two weeks. Once again, the opposition came not from the prosecution, but from the bench. I pointed to the number of lawyers from the attorney general's department appearing for the crown, and the difficulty of obtaining defence at such short notice. Eventually, it was postponed for further argument till the next day, and permission granted to me to see the prisoners that evening as I had to return to Nairobi.

I was taken under heavy guard, that is, I was driven in a jeep full of armed soldiers with a helicopter flying overhead, through a pass in the hills where the cold was felt in every part of my body. We stopped some distance away from what looked like a camp. I was told to alight and follow the soldiers, while a barbed-wire barricade was removed. Then I walked some two hundred feet along an asphalt path — soldiers behind and ahead. Suddenly a shout, followed by others, from both sides of the path, shook me. I will remember it as long as I live.

"Dudley, I am here — thank God — over here." I looked around, unable to find the source but able to recognize the voice of Kenyatta and others. The sound seemed to come from out of the ground. I stopped and looked around until I saw that there was some shadowy movement behind a slit in what appeared to be a concrete slab, about two feet off the ground. Their cells were below ground level with a small slit for air and light. They resembled the old tank traps used during the war. The cries were such that I was close to tears. There were cries of relief, like that of men under siege being relieved. It gave me new life. One can only imagine what it did for them. At last they were assured that word had gotten through and they were no longer alone. The outside world was aware of their existence and plight.

They shouted with joy when I was taken down to their cells, and they hugged me with unbelievable happiness. Somehow I forgot my weariness. There were unashamed tears in many eyes and everyone began talking at once. They all wanted to know what was happening in Kenya. Bits of gossip had come to them from prison workers, but they were more confusing than accurate. Jomo had tears in his eyes and his embrace was as strong as ever. He still wore his leather jacket, but they had taken away his beaded belt, his walking stick and large ring — which had all together been his hallmark, his constant dress. I told him that I would be back the next day and that I felt confident of success with my application. I would send abroad for the best lawyers. He gave me the name of two Indian lawyers. One, referred to earlier, had already responded negatively. The other, Achroo Kapila, was a very bright young Nairobi lawyer. He came back with me the following day and was of great help throughout the trial. It was only when I told the court that counsel had been contacted abroad and would be coming to lead the defence, and that immigration regulations required several days for immunization, that — with the support of Somerhough — we managed to get an adjournment for two weeks.

I went home to Moshi and cabled for assistance, as I could not depend on the postal services in Kenya. I sent cables to Norman Manley, Q.C., in Jamaica, Sir Hartley Shawcross, Q.C., ex-attorney general in Britain, and D. N. Pritt, Q.C., of the House of Commons. I had not the faintest idea how they would be paid. I also cabled Kwame Nkrumah in Ghana and Pandit Nehru in India explaining our difficulties. Shawcross's office replied that he was engaged in an oil dispute in Aden. N. W. Manley asked for more details as to the nature of the charges, length and date of trial. D. N. Pritt in a typical manner replied: "Will accept. Prepare to meet me in Nairobi." Later Kwame sent two lawyers, and Nehru sent five including Diwan Chawan Lall, an expert on the Law of Evidence with a high degree of practice. He had been an ambassador to Turkey.

The immigration office in Nairobi created problems. Of the African and Indian lawyers, only H. O. Davies, from Nigeria, and Diwan Lall, who had diplomatic immunity, were allowed into the country, the former because he managed to slip through unnoticed as an African. I tried to get the support of the Indian community in Nairobi to pressure the immigration office into allowing their fellow men into the country, but it was not forthcoming. The immigration officer in charge told me that the "gang of lawyers" already there was enough.

Pritt was the first to arrive. He had no difficulty. He had been a Member of Parliament for fifteen years and had had much experience in political trials. A long-time opponent of imperialism, and lawyer of outstanding international reputation, Pritt's unexpected appearance at Kapenguria not only embarrassed the colonial government but turned a small farcical show of justice into an international event. The distinguished team of lawyers I had gathered in defence of Jomo Kenyatta was far beyond anything the government had imagined in its plan to quickly convict and jail the KAU leaders.

Pritt had the heart of a lion. He impressed me from the start, and I can easily say after some forty years of practice I have never seen anyone more courageous and learned at the bar than he. I learned much from him. He was over sixty at the time and his mind was razor-sharp. With a dry sense of humour, he kept the team in high spirits throughout the case — even when on one occasion he was cited for contempt of court. Newsmen followed him around constantly in Kapenguria, always hoping to interview him and occasionally catching one of his many witticisms. Very early, he sized up the situation. He had a photographic memory and only had to read a document once to reproduce its contents with remarkable accuracy. Throughout the case he showed such superiority in his knowledge of the law over that of the judge that it produced a striking and pathetic picture. Somerhough, himself a good lawyer, appreciated Pritt's brilliance, and altogether they got along quite well. Pritt had one weakness — being hard of hearing he could not whisper, and many of his "hushed" witticisms, meant only for our ears, were heard through the entire court.

I recall one occasion in which Pritt objected to certain charges brought against one of the accused. Paul Ngei had been charged with using violent language against his arresting officers. Apparently he had been quite disorderly and had shouted something about the British not honouring their word. Pritt said this was not relevant to the case, while the judge argued that it was, that it showed he was the kind of man who would do violence to innocent Europeans. Pritt, under his breath — or as he thought, under his breath — said, "Well, there are many of us who would be put away for life if we said what we thought of the British in the colonies." The whole court heard it and there was a roar of laughter. It was a great pleasure and an education to watch him in action. His cut and thrust in debate was fearless. It was like watching a gladiator at his best in the arena.

As leader of the team, Pritt divided up the work as follows. Chaman Lall would follow up on all the legal points of evidence; on this he was an expert and had written a book on the Indian Evidence Act which we used. Pritt and H. O. Davies would lead our main witnesses and take their cross-examinations. Kapila, a brilliant Indian lawyer from Nairobi who took most of the notes, had to be absent on certain days when he returned to his practice there. Another filled in for him then. I was kept busy finding and interviewing witnesses, taking their statements, explaining the significance of local customs, researching points of law, or bringing authorities as precedents from the law library in Nairobi. It entailed hundreds of miles of travel each day, and at the end of the day there were joint consultations where, led by Pritt, we reviewed the day's work and planned for the morrow's. This conference usually took place on the verandah of Pritt's hotel before we all left him to drive back to our own havens of rest. The only hotel, as mentioned earlier, was for "whites only," so only Pritt was allowed to stay there. Indeed we all had to use our strongest persuasion to get this brave old warrior to accept it. Some weekends he drove the three hundred miles to Nairobi with me, to do some reading in the excellent law library there. Wherever we went, the judges and lawyers treated him with the greatest respect, in recognition of his many and eminent years at the bar. The white planters, however, expressed themselves differently. At one stage, the authorities had to intervene to prevent the farmers from staging a boycott against Pritt's hotel: they had refused to supply milk as long as he stayed there. No one at the hotel spoke to him, but he couldn't have cared less. Dismissing the whole thing with typical humour, he said: "It keeps my mind free from contamination."

Diwan Chaman Lall came with messages of goodwill from Nehru. On landing he had wanted to meet Jomo and deliver these messages personally, and it was there in Jomo's cell that a rather interesting exchange took place between them.

After I introduced him to Kenyatta and he conveyed best wishes from Nehru, Lall expressed the hope that after the case, when Jomo was free, they should form a closer African/Asian society as a political movement in Kenya. Jomo, the prisoner but still very much the man in charge and on centre stage, listened quietly throughout and then said: "Ask Dudley. We have several times spoken on this topic." Somewhat abashed, I had the difficulty of explaining that the majority of Indians in Kenya were a long distance away from the progressive views of Indians like Nehru. I had to describe them, with a few notable exceptions, as being the real leeches in Africa, taking as much as they could and leaving nothing in return. To make my point, I was even drawn to compare them with the colonialists! "If the British were to leave tomorrow," I said, "they would leave their parliamentary system, their laws and courts, and even their language, which has partly been adopted. But should the Indians leave, not a trace would be left behind save the few mansions they have built, which are only ever entered by Africans as servants through the back door." He was much taken aback and promised to give the matter serious consideration when he spoke to Indian leaders in Nairobi. Jomo added that he had not entered or even been invited to more than three Indian homes in all his time in Nairobi. One was that of J. M. Desai, a friend of mine, who gladly invited Jomo when I asked him. On the whole, they played a completely negative role in the liberation struggle, with the outstanding exception of Achroo Kapila and Makan Singh, who spent years in prison opposing the British imperialists.

Seeking out witnesses was a matter of some difficulty and often great danger. More often than not, those Africans needed lived deep in the village reserves. Some were afraid to come forward, especially since the police put every hindrance in the way of the defence. I had to take an interpreter, and in this role as in others Pio Pinto, a Goan Indian, proved an indefatigable worker. He worked day and night. I would tell him who or what I required and he would meet me with the desired information, statement or witness. After Kenya's independence, Pio came to an untimely death by assassination which, unfortunately, was all too common in the early history of independent Kenya. He had been given a junior minister's post in the government.

Kenyatta's arrest had sent ripples far and wide throughout the already troubled colony, and Mau Mau violence increased. The first European victim, Eric Bower, was chopped to death with *pangas* one week after Kenyatta's arrest. A month later an elderly European couple were attacked by a gang of men with *pangas* who entered their home on the edge of the Aberdare Forest — the husband was killed while assembling his shotgun; the wife, covered with blood managed to drive away for help. For the next several years — throughout Kenyatta's imprisonment — the Mau Mau would maintain a paramilitary base in the depths of the Aberdare. With Kenyatta's arrest the war in Kenya had really begun.

Joint military-police stations at this time began to run friendly competitions as to which had shot the most Kikuyu in a week. They proudly displayed the number of casualties chalked up in the bar or mess hall. A body count was made, and for them it was a happy hunting season. As tales multiplied of Mau Mau murders, the armament stores (open to Europeans only) did a thriving business. The traditional work of the white hunter assumed a far more sinister role in this famous safari country.

The Kikuyu felt their world crumbling. Any time of day or night they could be, and often were, awakened by soldiers or police and arrested or detained. It was not unusual for a whole village to be awakened in this way by soldiers and police surrounding their huts, searching and taking away men and women, often leaving small children frightened and crying, and babies alone, unprotected.

As the administration became more and more frustrated at their inability to stop Mau Mau activities, these village arrests became more frequent. I protested personally and vigorously to the colonial secretary when he came on a tour of inspection from London. It was patently clear that the arrest of an entire village was punitive and unjust, bound to include innocent women and children. The evil was further compounded when those arrested were put to forced labour. From time to time I saw women and children hauling logs, breaking stones, repairing roads, while supervised by armed guards. His reply was, "Thompson, we're living through difficult times. They demand rigorous remedies."

To fully realize the shattering effect that all this had on the African population, we have but to recall the exquisitely peaceful tenor of their lives before this inquisition. They had tilled the land, thatched their huts and tended their goats and cows. The women sang traditional songs while working in the fields, usually with babies strapped to their backs, showing only their heads bobbing up and down to the rhythm of the mother's movements. Here they would be busy pounding maize in the mortars in the open doorway of their huts, while their children amused themselves outside among the hens and dogs. It was, in the old days, an exceptional thing to see a policeman in the village. Now this peaceful fabric of domestic bliss and security had been ripped apart. Fear and silence took its place. But it was this silence, an apparent acquiescence to the brutal oppression, that proved victorious ultimately.

The European population suffered greatly too, from the very fear which they had themselves engendered. Young white boys and girls carried revolvers at their sides. They walked about in groups. These same children who had been reared by Kikuyu wet-nurses from earliest infancy, coddled and cared for, now walked in daily fear of every African. Europeans began to mistrust lifelong servants. The white mothers at home, especially on isolated farms, lived in fear all day while their husbands were at work, and the husbands at work could not give of their best, being preoccupied by fear for their families. These fears grew and spread among them as stories, mostly untrue, multiplied about Mau Mau atrocities, slaughter and mutilation. At home, guns were taken even into the bath. Europeans were living in constant dread in their own homes for fear their servants would suddenly become murderers and slay them asleep in bed, at the table or just sitting on their couches. Many began returning "home" to England, even those born in Kenya. Faces were gaunt and the effects of fear and tension showed everywhere. Suspicion lurked in eyes grown tired with waiting. It was a war of nerves for the Europeans. Their morale ebbed and their desperation showed itself in even more savage acts of repression against the Kikuyu. They became suspicious of every African.

I was told by a white friend in Nairobi that one day in his office a large book fell noisily to the floor. In an instant, nearly half a dozen pistols were drawn, and nearly a dozen Europeans rushed in a panic to get through the door.

But it was far worse for the hundreds of innocent Kikuyu who were harassed every day on their way to work and disturbed at night by sudden searches. Parliamentarians visited Kenya and strongly criticized the injustices they saw. Clement Davies, Leader of the Liberal Party, condemned the collective punishment as barbarous. "Nothing," he declared, "embittered people more than undeserved punishment inflicted on women and children."

In my effort to find witnesses for the defence, I discovered many cases where Africans had been intimidated and tortured by the authorities — mainly by the Kenyan police. One such case was that of Fred Mungai's wife. Mungai had been detained about the same time as Kenyatta. He was a trade union leader at the time of the emergency and had been the first African to call a strike in his district near Mombasa. I was very fond of him. He was a huge giant of a man with a head which would have been a sculptor's dream. His strong personality vibrated warmly out of his handsome features.

His friend, Kubai, whom I visited at Kapenguria, told me one day of his fear that Mungai's wife was being harassed. Mungai had long been imprisoned elsewhere and was not there to protect her. Kubai told me that this was affecting him greatly as they had all been the closest of friends. I promised him that on my return to Nairobi I would investigate the matter personally. It was very moving to see this strong man, a political prisoner, sympathizing with a situation so many miles away, the predicament of a friend's wife, while he himself was under such severe restraint.

On following up the matter, I witnessed something I shall never forget and find it impossible to forgive. The district was not very well known to me; I was viewed as a stranger and had to pursue my objective with the utmost caution, if not guile.

As I moved from hut to hut and bar to bar quietly asking the whereabouts of Bibi wa Mungai (Mungai's wife), I met the stony response, *"si jui"* ("I don't know"). After a few days of doing this, a young man came up to me. I had been noticed and indeed closely watched. He wanted to know who I was asking for and why. Satisfying himself that I was really there to help and that I was not acting for the police, he told me to follow him. He led me along a very winding trail to a large open hut. It was really only a circular thatched roof supported by wooden poles and without walls. Inside, many Africans were drinking local beer or *pombe*. It should be pointed out here that Africans were not allowed, "for their own protection," to buy hard liquor, or to enter European bars without being given individual permission and a licence by the district commissioner. As a result, African areas had their own bars where beer, brewed from banana or peanuts or some other locally prevailing crop, was sold. Most of these were run by women, known as *pombe* queens, who accumulated much wealth as a result. When I entered I felt the drinking and conversation come to a halt as I was scrutinized by everyone. I was led to a table where the *pombe* queen sat on a stool, two hundred and odd pounds of sober strength. She wiped the sweat from her forehead in one sweeping movement of her arm, which was almost as wide as my waist, and looking me straight in the eye, she said *"Jambo."* Her colourful gown, tucked under her arms, revealed mighty but smooth shoulders. Her earrings were beaded circles about four inches in diameter: they would have seemed oversized on any other woman. She spoke without smiling. I returned the salutation, doing my best to look pleasant. Then there was a rapid exchange between herself and my guide in a language unknown to me, but I distinctly heard the name "Mungai" mentioned. His tone seemed to commend me. She returned her inscrutable gaze once more and handed me a drink which she scooped with a practised hand out of a gigantic copper pot using a ladle of calabash gourd. I accepted the drink. It was a sign not only of African hospitality, but of trust. She said *"Aikombe,"* and I put the calabash to my lips and said, *"Riambe,"* then passed it back to her. It was a ritual I already knew. The drink first had to be tasted by the one who offered it, a custom which might have originated when poison potions quickly dispatched enemies.

After this, I was approached by an elder, a white-bearded and very old man with a robe thrown over his shoulder. He brought his face very close to mine, squinting through half-closed eyes. Suddenly he dropped his cane and flung both arms around me and began chattering in a tongue which I recognized as Kikuyu. There was an immediate relaxation of tension and one of the crowd spoke out in Swahili: *"Wewe ni Bwana wakili Thompson was Moshi"* ("You are lawyer Thompson from Moshi"). This was greeted with much satisfaction in the bar, and the serious drinking commenced with vigour and noise. The *pombe* queen broke into a smile, revealing a perfect set of ivory teeth which transformed her face into one of utter beauty. My drink made from fermented bananas tasted like smoky water, but I swallowed it with a smile that would have stopped a spear in flight. She asked me, *"Unataka Kumwana bibi wa ya Bwana Mungai?"* ("Do you want to see Mungai's wife?"). She spoke to two young men in the Kikuyu language who immediately beckoned to me, *"Njoo"* ("Come"). I followed them along a track similar to the first, leaving the crowd that had resumed their drinking and talking louder than before. They now had a new topic to talk about — a man who was Black but not an African, who spoke and dressed like a European. That would no doubt provide a talking point for a very long time to come.

After a walk of less than ten minutes in the bright sunlight, we came to a hut. The guides entered by removing the cowskin which served as a screen as well as a door. They waved me in by a motion of the hand. There was no window inside, and it took some time for my eyes to make out anything in this darkness after being in the bright sunlight. There was total silence within. Gradually, as my eyes became accustomed, I made out a bed. An old bearded man, probably a traditional healer, stood motionless at the foot of the bed in utter disregard of the intruders. He stood like a sentinel guarding a grave. One of the men moved forward and uncovered the naked body of a mutilated woman — Mungai's wife. At first she seemed a corpse. She neither moved nor uttered a sound. I went closer and bent over her. She was breathing but had not opened her eyes. Eventually I spoke: *"Nina barua wa Bwana Fred Mungai"* ("I have a message from Mister Fred Mungai"). The word *"Bwana,"* which is not easily rendered in English, implies respect, and assured her that it was a message of goodwill. She turned her head slowly and said, almost in a whisper: *"Jambo, habari gani?"* ("Hello, what news do you bring?").

I replied in Swahili that her husband was well and that he was thinking of her constantly, that he had heard she was not well and, as he could not come himself, had asked me to do so and to report to him.

She smiled weakly and replied: "I am glad to hear that he is well. I too am thinking of him and hope he will soon return."

I asked her if she had been imprisoned, but she merely closed her eyes without replying. One of the young men pointed to her breasts, and I bent closer to examine the marks on her body. There were multiple wounds of a similar pattern all over her swollen breasts and the wounds were pus-infected. It was later explained to me that part of the torture she underwent was having her breasts squeezed and pulled with mechanical pliers. Her genitals were also disfigured. The last words I heard from this poor Kikuyu woman, spoken just above a whisper, was a message to her Fred: "Tell him I never answered their questions." Some time later I was told that this faithful woman never recovered. She went insane and died on her bed of suffering. She never saw her husband again.

Torture related to

Mau Mau

In this barbarism and counter barbarism there were many ugly and painful scenes. Atrocity begat atrocity and violence returned violence. The Kikuyu singled out for respect and friendship the Quakers who worked as missionaries among them. It was a Quaker working at a hospital who sent for me to come and see the condition of some of the maltreated Kikuyu. He was prepared to go to court to give evidence that men and women were brought to the hospital so badly beaten that pieces of their skin and flesh remained behind on the floors of the trucks in which they were delivered. Many had been beaten with the *kiboko* or rhinoceros-hide whip. The hospitals were full, and could barely accommodate them, even lying on the floor.

Now let us return to the trial of Jomo Kenyatta. A few days after the trial actually began, when Pritt and myself were alone discussing a point of law, he said to me, as a teacher would to a pupil: "Dudley, you know of course they are all going to be convicted?"

I was shocked. "Why do you say that? Haven't you got any confidence in our case?"

He smiled, "Don't let this observation lessen your ardour one bit. This is a political trial if ever I saw one. We're only going through the motions for public consumption to reinforce faith in the justice of British jurisprudence." In my innocence, I did not understand his term "political trial." "Do you remember the Reichstag Fire trial in Berlin?" he asked. "Well, It's exactly the same here in Kapenguria. The government is determined to have their heads. Prepare for it but don't let it deter you from putting in your best. At least we can expose the system." I began to understand him and to respect him all the more. His formidable defence revealed none of his preconceptions. The nearest he came to voicing his opinion was as he was boarding the plane for London just before the verdict, which was reserved by the judge (to give the impression of serious consideration). The newsmen who always followed him around asked for his farewell opinion on the outcome of the case. Pritt, with some folders under one arm and a briefcase in the other, turned slowly at the top of the stairs and said: "Well, gentlemen, if Great Britain is trying to break up her empire, she certainly is going about it in the right way."

The trial was a farce. There was not a scintilla of evidence to demonstrate that Kenyatta advocated or encouraged any but legitimate means to obtain justice and freedom for his people. Throughout the proceedings the defence team was kept completely in the dark as to the particulars of the case. We knew that Kenyatta was charged with leading and managing the Mau Mau and that there were some sixteen other counts against him, but when we asked for particulars (in what way — when — how — was he leading the Mau Mau?) the judge stolidly refused to comply with our requests. We would go to court not knowing what charges we were up against. Only when the prosecution called its witnesses and it was stated: "On the fifth of January so and so was seen . . . ," and so forth, would we know what was going on. Then we would constantly have to defer cross-examining until we could go and check those particulars.

Ironically enough, at the opening of the case the prosecution went to great lengths to emphasize that "this is not a political trial." As I heard Mr. Somerhough repeat this several times and indicate with derisory gestures that the six men accused should be considered as pickpockets or common thieves, it struck me that the gentleman did "protest too much," and was clearly trying to convince himself. No one could do other than realize that history was being made. There were the six accused — all national figures of importance. The mere presence of Pritt and the other distinguished lawyers propelled the case onto the international stage of events.

The six accused presented a varying picture. All belonged to the executive of the KAU. It was an obvious ploy to decapitate that organization which was the only vehicle through which Africans could vent their frustration with the government. This alone reveals the short-sightedness of the administration. The pent up feelings and growing impatience of hundreds of thousands of Africans was bound to go underground if their one legitimate means of expression was silenced. I had known all these men for some time, in different capacities. Jomo I had been closest to over the years. The others I met in Kenya, usually at the headquarters of the KAU in Nairobi, at social functions or meetings.

Fred Kubai, one of the six, was a tall and burly individual. His thick black beard barely revealed the smile he wore easily and often. He was a trade union leader, and fearless, and had led an early strike in Kenya. Of all the accused he was particularly detested by the white plantocracy. Bildad Kaggia was a man with whom I spent many hours in conversation. He was a much smaller man, in build, than Kubai, and had travelled to Britain as a soldier. He spoke English quite well. We had long arguments about religion, his chief interest. He was deeply religious and believed that the European settlers had twisted Christianity to become an instrument of oppression. "Look," he said to me, "they have a white church and a white God. My God, who must be different from theirs, would have a hard time being admitted into their church."

Paul Ngei, another of the accused, was a tall, exceptionally handsome man. His temper was quick and he expressed his contempt for the entire colonial system quite freely. He was not a Kikuyu. An able and ambitious man, he, like Kubai, came to visit me in Jamaica in later years. After Kenya's independence he was given a cabinet post. A man used to the good life, he once entertained a delegation from Jamaica in his lovely home. His bearing was military and he had appeared in several films made in Africa by European film-makers. A unique personality during the trial was that of Achieng Oneko. Tall, mercurial, he was always moving and appeared to be the youngest in the group. His intelligence was quick. He was always neatly dressed, very alive and ready for conversation. His slanted eyes and high cheekbones made him look Oriental. I would tease him about this, calling him a "Black Chinese sage." After the appeal Oneko was released, but then again detained under the Emergency Laws. After independence he was made minister of information.

The last of the accused was Kungu Karumba, and he was very different from the others. He was the only one who was not literate. He had cataracts in both eyes and was nearly blind. He spoke very little and always Kikuyu, although he understood Swahili. Throughout the trial he sat quietly and seemed very far away. A man of medium height and of middle age, he was of hardworking peasant stock.

The crown's case against all the accused, as stated by Somerhough on the first day of the trial, was that Mau Mau, an unlawful society, was a militant branch of the Kenya African Union. The crown claimed that they had fourteen witnesses for the prosecution — they ended up bringing in over forty. They had absolutely no case. Much of the evidence brought in to tie Kenyatta to the Mau Mau rituals, pointed to times when he was not even in Kenya, or to times before the society had been outlawed. It therefore could not be properly related to any charge. My honest feeling about any link between the KAU and Mau Mau was (and still is) that Kenyatta was not involved, and the KAU was not a branch of the Mau Mau, but that there were two among the accused whom I am almost sure were at one time or another involved in the secret society. However, evidence to prove this was never presented to the court.

The very first witness for the prosecution was a man named Rawson Mcharia who had once been a neighbour of Kenyatta. He claimed that Kenyatta had personally administered a Mau Mau oath to several people while he was present and that Kenyatta had tried to make Mcharia also take the oath. The date of this incident was given as March 1950. Mau Mau was not then an outlawed society and Pritt argued that the evidence be disallowed. Thacker accepted it, however, on the grounds that it indicated the possibility of Kenyatta's taking part in such ceremonies after they became outlawed.

Six years after the trial, this witness, Mcharia, signed an affidavit swearing that his evidence against Kenyatta was untruthful and that he had been given, in return for this fabricated evidence, air fare to London, enough money for a two-year course at a British university, enough subsistence for himself and his family, and the offer of a government post on his return. He did go to Britain on the scholarship and was paid as stated.

Montague Slater's book *The Trial of Jomo Kenyatta* analyses the trial in detail, and those wishing to look further into the case should consult that text. It is enough to say that though the trial went on for some fifty-eight days, it was evident to us from day one that the crown had no case, and the trial was intrinsically unfair. Not only the judge, but the court interpreter, was obviously biased. He was none other than L. S. B. Leakey, an old opponent of Kenyatta's. The courtroom atmosphere was blatantly hostile. Only white officials and farmers and their wives were allowed in, and there was considerable cheering whenever the crown's witnesses said anything against the accused. It seemed at times to be the scene of a lynching rather than a court of law.

One witness for the crown claimed, like Mcharia, that he had seen Kenyatta at an oath-taking ceremony. Not only that, but he gave the names of ten other people who were with him at the time, who he said also witnessed this. The crown, when asked to produce these witnesses, gave various reasons as to why they could not be present. We found all ten and they refuted everything the crown's witness had said. One of them even brought his diary and showed that on the dates he was said to have witnessed the accused's actions, he was somewhere else. Judge Thacker said: "I believe the witness for the crown; I disbelieve all ten of these witnesses for the defence."

One day I came across a young English lawyer who had recently come to Africa as a magistrate. We had known each other in England as students and he invited me for a drink. He said, "Dudley, I don't know how you stand it." I nodded. Then he continued, "These Africans coming up for trial day after day all swearing innocence." I continued drinking. "And we have to go through an entire trial knowing all the time the bastards are guilty." I asked to be excused. I had misjudged my old friend and he had misjudged me: he had already joined the judicial murder factory in East Africa.

There had been fundamental changes in the laws of evidence made during this trial. In some cases witnesses gave evidence with hoods over their heads to hide their identities, and their names were not revealed in court. It is hard to cross-examine someone with a hood over his head, and our clients could not instruct us to counter the evidence: they could not say whether or not it was true that X had seen them in such and such a place, as they did not know who X was.

Mr. X would swear he had attended a certain illegal meeting as a police informer, and give details as to how many men and women were naked, which calabash held the goat's blood and describe other details of the Mau Mau ritual, before pointing to the accused. The accused on the other hand could only flatly deny it without being in a real position to prove he had never been in the company of the witness. Further, there was admitted what was called "affidavit evidence" where a police officer could read in court an affidavit sworn to him by an unnamed witness who would not appear.

There was also the case where two European officers swore an oath saying that they had searched a certain farm and found two used cartridge shells in the hut of the accused. This case was not at Kapenguria, but was one of many trials in other parts of Kenya where I defended alleged members of the Mau Mau. In this case, the accused was sentenced to death. I was absolutely certain that he was innocent of any involvement with the Mau Mau: he was simply a Kikuyu farm-worker. Before donning the black cap which is part of the ritual of sentencing a man to death, the judge called out, as usual: "Is there anything you wish to say before sentence is passed upon you?" The accused usually stood silently. This time the injustice was so flagrant that I was moved to speak on his behalf. I looked around the courtroom and saw the resigned looks of other Kikuyu men and women all awaiting their sentences, and of the others looking in from outside, helpless and mistreated in their own land and I said: "Yes, my Lord."

"What is it that you have to say, Mr. Thompson?" "In my country, my Lord," and I thought of Kingston far away over the seas and I felt suddenly helpless and alone, "there is a saying that 'Time is longer than rope.'"

"What does that mean? What are you getting at?" and he snatched off his glasses angrily, hoping to lure me into committing a contempt of court.

"It means, my Lord, that your jurisdiction over this man is merely limited to the rope by which you may hang him. But there are millions whose deeds can only be measured by history in the years to come, and time, my Lord, is longer than rope."

He was sentenced to be hanged by the neck till dead. I appealed, and several months later while the accused was patiently waiting in the con-demned cell, I was able to prove to the Court of Appeal from immigration records, that the two officers who gave fabricated evidence against him were not in Kenya at the time when they "discovered" the cartridges in the accused's hut. He was released from death row, but like many others, including Koinange, as soon as he was released from prison, he was

detained under emergency regulations. As this detention took place immediately outside the court house, the accused, although he had had his life
restored to him, would still not be able to see his family for a very long
time. It was my belief that, in every case of appeal, the police had blank
detention forms ready to hand out if the appeals, as they often did, went
against them.

During this period, while the so called "ring leaders" were in detention
or in prison, there was no lull in the brutalities taking place. The police still
kept their score of body counts; the torture and slaughter continued. It was
plain, bloody war.

I ran into Geoffrey, my lawyer friend from Oxford, again. It had only
been a month or two since I had last seen him, but he appeared haggard.
Once more he invited me for a drink and we got in his car. As he drove he
rattled on: "This blasted place — it's rockers," he said, "crazy. I don't know
what's happening; every night I expect not to wake up alive." He drove
very fast and seemed to have forgotten our original mission. He began
telling me of the "butchery" he had witnessed: "I saw the police set fire to
those huts and the soldiers shoot them down like rabbits when they ran out.
Jesus, one woman was cut down with a baby in her arms, and they went
over and shot the baby. I threw up all over the place." I kept silent in
sympathy with him. "Nine days ago," he continued, "an entire farm at
Nyeri, massacred. The farmer came home and found his wife, the servants,
all butchered, even the dog. When is it all going to stop? I don't know who
to trust anymore. Dudley, I'm quitting. I'm going home. There's no sanity
anywhere. We can't kill them all — so what's the use?"

His words, his questions, kept pounding in my head for days. When was
it all going to stop? I began to think the lucky ones were those in the
detention stockades. I had heard of Josephine Muthoni's arrest. She had
been identified with us as she had lent two of her cars to the defence team.
The authorities found this out when Pritt had an accident. He was forced
off the road, but fortunately ended up only with a few bruises. The car he
was driving in was traced to Josephine, and she was suddenly taken into
custody, and disappeared with the rest of those "missing." Weeks later I
heard that she was at the stockade of Kajiaado. I got permission to talk
with her in the presence of her jailor — he turned out to be more humane
than most. Josephine told me of conditions in the camp and asked about
her children. I assured her all was well. She said that most of the guards
could be bribed, so I left money with her. She called to the jailor and spoke
to him in Kikuyu. Apparently a child had been born in the camp and had
been without clothes for days. The mother had very little milk and the child

had been ill. The jailor accepted the money and was quite willing to buy milk and clothes for the child and to give special attention to Josephine. I visited the camp several times and often took in bottles of brandy, medicine, cheese and bars of chocolate, along with money, which helped to pave the way to better treatment. One thing which impressed me was the strict discipline and behaviour self-imposed by the prisoners. The jailers told me that there was not a single case of violation or molestation, though conditions were so far from ideal and the camp was overcrowded.

I also paid regular visits to Jomo and the others during the trial. He was kept fully informed of what was taking place in the country. On one occasion he was advised by me to select three party officers for the KAU, each one to succeed the other, as the arrest factor was so high. It was on one such occasion that I introduced to him the name of Tom Mboya, already referred to. I was often the go-between for Jomo and his followers who still accepted his word as law.

One day before a visit to Kenyatta I saw in the Kenya newspaper something which completely shocked me. There was a picture of a blonde boy of about five years old, riding a bicycle. He had that smile of innocence only a child can wear. The article detailed how he had been murdered, brutally slain by the Mau Mau along with his sister aged seven, his mother and father. The house servants were all missing, save one who had obviously put up fierce resistance. The police were on a manhunt for their killers and no doubt hundreds would be arrested "in connection with the crime."

It shocked me, not only because of the senseless slaying of the children, but more so as I had known the family well. They were the Rucks, a young and very popular family, and I had enjoyed their hospitality many times. Mrs. Ruck, an English nurse, had kept a dispensary where she often attended to the wounds of the Africans living nearby. They had both been entirely sympathetic to the Kikuyu case. It was a terrible tragedy, and the African newspapers made much of it. They described how the adults were hacked to death as they ran and struggled across their front lawn, how bloodied strands of Mrs. Rucks' blonde hair had been found strewn across the grass as she tried to escape her murderers, and how, having completed their savagery on the couple, they killed the children who were hiding in their room.

I was enraged on reading this, and I took the paper into the cell and showed Kenyatta. He too was shocked. He shook his head several times and said: "They were our friends. Tell them to find out who did it and punish them."

I said, "Jomo, this is bad. I no longer feel safe here. They have gone mad."

He said, "No Dudley, this is war. If I were not here in jail, it wouldn't have happened. Go tell them what I say."

I later met, in great secrecy, with members of the Mau Mau. They blindfolded me and took me along a winding bushy path in the hills. I showed them the picture of the Rucks and gave them Jomo's instructions. They sat silently around a fire. I saw no sympathy. They were unmoved. No one seemed to understand my complaint. I said, "If Mau Mau could do this to them, they could as easily kill me. These people were helping us. I no longer feel safe here."

A whisper passed among them like the soft rustling of leaves and then one of the leaders spoke, and it was translated for me: "Tell Jomo, it will be done. But you are not like them. You are our brother," and then he added what can only be a definition of total war: "Sometimes you have to kill the best ones first, lest we ourselves weaken in the struggle."

As I left there I thought, "Is there always going to be this perpetual hate between races?"

The Lari Massacre was the glaring example of the brutal warfare the Mau Mau were now engaged in. For months warnings had been given by the Mau Mau that "loyalists" should cease oppressing their Kikuyu brothers. In particular they were warned not to accept confiscated land as the reward for such action. Lari was a village consisting of confiscated lands which had been given to some of the loyalists. One morning, Kenya awakened to find it the scene of a bloody massacre. Men, women and children, had been slaughtered overnight. Several African police perished. Not a single shot had been fired. They were all slain with *pangas* as they slept. Even animals were slaughtered, and the avengers had all disappeared like shadows into the forest before the dawn revealed the awful sight.

That same night there was a raid on a police station at Naivasha. The Mau Mau, with only a few guns among them, raided the station for ammunition and got away in government trucks which they drove into the forests. These two incidents at Lari and Naivasha occurred in the last weeks of the trial and turned European sentiments even further against Kenyatta. Kenyatta, on the other hand, was unable at this final stage to say anything to restrain those militants in the Aberdare forests who had turned Mau Mau into a full-fledged liberation struggle. Somerhough had accused Kenyatta of never having truly denounced the Mau Mau.

SOMERHOUGH: You will agree that your so-called denunciation has had very little effect at all?

KENYATTA: That is a lie.

SOMERHOUGH: You think it has?

KENYATTA: It has, yes.

SOMERHOUGH: You think Mau Mau is better since you started denouncing it?

It should be noted that the crown, assisted by Leakey, had tried to prove that Kenyatta's message to the people at Kiambu, when he had denounced Mau Mau, was filled with "underlying meanings" — the opposite to what he said — which only the Kikuyu would understand. Kenyatta, undergoing this examination by the crown, spoke up:

KENYATTA: You people have the audacity to ask me silly questions. I have done my best and if all people had done as I have done, Mau Mau would not be as it is now. You made it what it is, not Kenyatta.

SOMERHOUGH: What — 'You Europeans,' the crown or who — made it what it is?

KENYATTA: The government is not handling Mau Mau in the proper way and you blame it on me.

SOMERHOUGH: It is the government's fault that Mau Mau exists and goes on?

KENYATTA: Well I say yes.

At the closing of the crown's evidence against the accused, Pritt said that "this was the most childishly weak case made against any man in any important trial, in the history of the British empire." He had to leave Kenya early in March, a month before the final verdict and sentencing. In his closing speech he said: "Managing Mau Mau. . . . In what fashion, with what assistance, in what office, with what policy, with what documents? Never, never anything."

Judge Thacker sentenced Kenyatta to seven years hard labour, to be followed by indefinite restriction. It must be remembered that Kenyatta at this time was a man in his early sixties. He was found guilty of managing the Mau Mau and of "taking the fullest advantage of the power and influence which you have over your own people, and also of the primitive instincts which you know lie deep down in their characters."

In his closing statement Kenyatta said: ". . . we feel that this case has been so arranged as to make scapegoats of us in order to strangle the Kenya African Union, the only African political organization which fights for the rights of African people. We wish to say that what we have done in our activities has been to try our level best to find ways and means by which the community in this country can live in harmony. But what we have objected to — and we shall continue to object — are the discriminations in the government of this country. We shall not accept that, whether we are in jail or out of it, Sir, because we find that this world has been made for human beings to live in happily, to enjoy the good things and the produce of the country equally, and to enjoy the opportunities that this country has to offer."

Years later in his book *Suffering Without Bitterness,* Kenyatta commented on the trial:

"Of course there was no legal contest in Kapenguria between plaintiff and defendant of equal weight, as for example between nations with equal resources, or financial empires, or individuals of equal social force. . . . The defence had nothing more tangible than truth and justice."

Pritt spent the next few years trying to appeal the case. I visited Kenyatta in his prison at Lokitaung, petitioned to alleviate his harsh conditions, and also petitioned for his early release. In the meantime, each day saw the same savage stalemate in Kenya. It was not to be compared with guerilla warfare such as that of the freedom fighters in South and Central America. These can usually be plotted on maps in terms of campaign action, successes and losses, and one can usually estimate those areas under control. Here was a war of invisible terror everywhere. The guns were almost entirely on one side, with the exception of a few captured guns. A minimal number were smuggled into Kenya from Tanganyika. Crude homemade guns made from stolen bicycle tubing or any metal cylinders were used. The standard weapon however was the *panga,* a razor-sharp two-edged machete, said to be sharp enough to bisect a falling feather floating down on its own weight.

Occasionally there was an ambush of askaris, and guns, grenades and other equipment were acquired. Later in the campaign, guerilla leaders like General China and Dedan Kimathi organized well-planned raids on police stations. The most effective force was terror. Government forces could not fight shadows and so they satisfied themselves with the blood of innocent villagers. This was counter productive and drove more and more Kikuyu into the campaign on the side of the freedom fighters. It gave them a real cause, and many developed into ferocious bands of fighters for freedom against imperialist murderers and rapists. Things grew worse as the Mau Mau directed their warfare not only against the Europeans, but also the Kikuyu loyalists. On the other side, with the government forces continuing their own atrocities, those Kikuyu who refused to join the Home Guard or to inflict suffering on their own people, were classified as "terrorists" and themselves detained, tortured or killed.

The cost of war mounted. The economy was being severely affected, and many settlers began to leave for "home" or for South Africa. It became obvious as time went by that the government was in a no-win position. The British began to send out feelers, to open talks on constitutional reform. The hardcore, intransigent, white settler minority would not entertain the thought, and resisted every inch of the way. They even staged a demonstration against any negotiation with the Africans and marched against Government House.

In Operation Anvil on April 24, 1954, government forces put into effect their largest, and up to that point most drastic measure against the Kikuyu population. Over 30,000 Kikuyu were removed from their homes and sent to special camps, and Kikuyu land was sealed off from the rest of Kenya. With this, the fighting moved even further into the Aberdare forest, into areas found impenetrable by British and Kenyan troops. There, the Mau Mau maintained bases right up until Kenyatta's release in 1961, and some die-hards did not surrender the cause until Kenya's independence in 1963.

In 1952 Pritt returned to Kenya to appeal Kenyatta's case. At a hearing of the Supreme Court at Kitale it was discovered that Judge Thacker had been appointed to the wrong district during the Kapenguria trial. This technicality made the whole trial void, and Kenyatta was technically a free man. Hearing this, the settlers in Kitale went mad. They threatened to shoot Pritt, and the police had to smuggle him out of Kenya. A month later, the East Africa Court of Appeal reversed the Kitale judgement. Pritt continued to appeal in London, taking it to the Privy Council. In the summer of 1954, the Privy Council turned down the appeal. Pritt wrote of this later, "In the forty years in which I practised before the Privy Council, during which time I presented hundreds of petitions for special leave, I never had another case which was as strong as this one of Kenyatta."

Kenyatta was at this time in Lokitaung, a northern desert area where Sudan, Ethiopia and Kenya meet. The government, which had all along done everything in its power to promote the impression that this was a criminal, not a political, case, treated him as a common criminal, issuing him short prison trousers and an identification number, and for the first few months of imprisonment he wore chains around his ankles. After a while because of his age, he was released from hard labour and given the job of cooking for the others. All the prisoners lived in a shack with a corrugated tin roof and they slept on the hard cement floor. His guards were chosen from Africans not in sympathy with the Kikuyu.

Above and below, Jomo Kenyatta in detention, ca. 1954-1955;
below, a visit from his daughter, Margaret

I believe that the government of Kenya hoped to completely erase his memory from the minds of his people and have him die unnoticed in far Lokitaung. His home at Githunguru was destroyed, his family split up, and it is now known that a "new prisoner" was sent to Lokitaung to attack Kenyatta in prison. He might have succeeded in killing him, if not for the bravery of Paul Ngei — also imprisoned with Kenyatta — and some of the others who rescued Kenyatta. Over the years, a few minor concessions were made, to make life more bearable for the prisoners. Kenyatta was able to receive a limited number of visitors, and was overcome with joy when visited by his daughter, Margaret. I visited him a number of times, taking him news, books, letters and gifts.

In 1955, a few months before I left East Africa, a new District Commissioner, Lieutenant de Roebeck, took over at Lokitaung and things vastly improved for Kenyatta and the others. Up till then, their labour had consisted mainly in breaking stones. Roebeck allowed them to plant vegetable gardens. He also had them wash and iron their civilian clothes so that they would be in good condition when they were released. In short, he was decent enough to treat them as political prisoners serving an allotted time — not criminals shut away from society hopelessly. De Roebeck also gave permission for Kenyatta to give lessons in English to General China — that die-hard Mau Mau warrior.

In making formal requests for Kenyatta's early release I was told, "it was not in his own best interest," and on another occasion that he was "the prince of darkness and death." Meanwhile his reputation thrived among his people and overseas. His cause was now international. The groundswell in his favour, from the grassroots of Kenya to the outside world, increased Jomo's stature to larger-than-life size. East Africa and its clamour for Kenyatta's release were placed on the agenda of the world.

As much as the government had done to break the spirit and the popularity of Kenyatta, his personality remained indomitable. European visitors to Lokitaung were greeted personally by him at the gate, and then they were shown around the vegetable garden, in the manner of a delegation visiting the head of government at the State Palace. He would sit with me in that garden much the same way he had at Githinguru and, there against the background of uninhabited African desert, I knew I was in the presence of a truly great man.

In 1959 Kenyatta completed his term of imprisonment at Lokitaung. He was moved about ninety miles south to Lodwar to begin an indefinite period of restriction. Lodwar was another kind of imprisonment. He was not allowed to enter any private building and could move around freely only in about 800 yards of desert area. He was also given two hours a day to shop in specified shops, two Indian *dukas*. The pressure for his release continued to grow. New political parties had sprung up in Kenya, in particular the Kenya African Democratic Union, KADU, and it was incredible that despite efforts by the Kenyan authorities to pacify and/or divide these groups, they were united in the one dominant theme: "Free Kenyatta now."

Kenya's new governor, Sir Patrick Renison, proved to be particularly insensitive to the demands for Kenyatta's freedom and government reform. On one occasion he invited Tom Mboya and Ronal Mgala, who represented KANU and KADU respectively, to Government House. They were both under the impression that the governor was at last about to have dialogue on these topics. Instead, with a dramatic flourish, his excellency treated them to a recorded broadcast to the nation in which he said his position was unchanged. The two leaders disassociated themselves from the statement and requested to interview Kenyatta at Lodwar. This was refused. Eventually, around the last week in March of that year, they were given permission. They not only saw him as a joint delegation and brought him up to date with news, but also renewed their support for his release. Further, they used the occasion to record a message from him which they played at the All African People's Conference in Cairo a few days later. This was his message:

"This is Jomo Kenyatta speaking from Lodwar. I am very happy to send you my greeting and best wishes for the success of the conference. I hope the All African People's Conference will work for the unity and strength of our people everywhere. The time has come when Africa must with other nations show that she has something, not only to receive, but to give to the rest of the world. I hope peace and prosperity will come to our people, when all of us can write and work for the purpose of uplifting our people who have been struggling so hard for centuries."

The message from this great man had an electrifying effect among the members of the conference and led to increased pressure for his release.

In April 1961, Kenyatta and his family were flown from Lodwar to Maralel. This is a district half-way between Lodwar and Nairobi. Conditions here were better, though he was still under restriction. He remained here for about four months. While at Maralel, a large contingent of the international press, including television newsmen, cameramen and other reporters, visited him. They had a lengthy interview in which they canvassed his views on future developments, interracial relations, land questions, constitutional reform and a wide range of topics. Kenyatta showed himself to be the great statesman that he was, showing no sign of bitterness.

After many years of close friendship with him, I can easily say that his ability to forgive was one of his most outstanding characteristics. He forgave Mcharia, the chief witness against him, and offered him a plot of land. He forgave the judges who sentenced him and granted their application to remain in Kenya after independence. There are other cases I could cite. During the last years of his incarceration, KANU had been growing rapidly, always under the banner "Mzee Kenyatta." He was elected President, in absentia, and his friend James Gichuru, a school teacher, acted as his "locum tenens."

It was obvious when Kenyatta was moved to Maralel, that Governor Renison was preparing the country and himself for Kenyatta's liberation. The governor, a most stubborn and tactless individual, was reacting without grace to the mounting pressure of public opinion both inside and outside of the country. At Maralel there was an increasing procession of visitors to Kenyatta. They consisted of diplomats, professional men, politicians and leaders of various civic groups. They all left with glowing pictures of his unflinching courage and wisdom. In the House of Legislature, members did not relax for one moment in their request for his immediate release. One outstanding example of this was the maiden speech of Fitz DeSouza in May 1962. Mr. DeSouza had been part of the legal team at Kapenguria, and gave details in his speech to prove that the trial was a farce. Public opinion was such that the newspapers both in England and Kenya now wrote editorials demanding his release. Members of Parliament in England made it clear in their speeches that stability would not come to Kenya until this was done. Mr. Colin Legum wrote in the *Observer* on July 5, 1961:

The two month old attempt to carry Kenya forwards to Independence, while keeping Mr. Kenyatta in detention, has failed. It is now widely recognized that no real political progress can be made until Kenyatta has been released. In a sense, therefore, it appears that Kenya is Kenyatta's prisoner rather than the other way around.

Finally, the governor, in a very grudging statement, announced that Kenyatta would be released after nearly nine years of confinement. On August 14, 1961, Mzee Jomo Kenyatta was flown back to Nairobi, to a military airstrip near his home, and swept aloft in a motorcade with a strong police escort to keep off the tumultuous and joyous crowd. He was taken to Gatunda and for several days was besieged by a loving crowd, overwhelming in their expression of joy, relief and hope. Their protector had returned to them. The African champion was free.

9 Leaving East Africa

Kenyatta's release, and the movement of Kenya towards complete independence in 1963, occurred after I had left the country. In the summer of 1955 I prepared to leave East Africa for good and return to Jamaica. I could not say I was going "home," for a great part of me will always belong to that great continent. There was so much left there that I felt uncertain as to whether this was a permanent goodbye. Still, I had to succumb to the strong, growing demands of family ties. I wanted my children to be rooted in the West Indies, and in Jamaica in particular. They had to know their role, as I had known mine.

I was going back to Jamaica to start again from the bottom, strengthened by my experiences in Africa. Without such experience, I might not have been able to understand the problems, ambitions and hopes of the "real" people of my own country. Elsewhere I shall depict their struggle, which continues. It is a campaign against those who refuse to accept change and the full meaning and possibilities for all in a Third World independent country. I am fortunate to have received "the gift of sacrifice" which enabled me to work as I did in Africa, and then to assist my comrades who in those years of my absence had been struggling for some of those same rights in Jamaica.

My very last case in Africa was a memorable one involving a Masai herdsman. He had put a spear through a white farmer, a South African ex-veterinarian who had recently become a cattle farmer.

The defendant, Oldtus-Bin-Lisau ("Oldtus, son of a woman called Lisau"), was six-feet seven-inches. He was tremendously strong and well-built, wearing his cow-skin like a toga over one shoulder and carrying a spear. Oldtus didn't speak a word of English.

He was charged with murder. One unique characteristic of the Masai is that they will never tell a lie. They have a great problem understanding modern lawyers. They are going to tell the truth no matter what any lawyer or anyone else tells them to say. You can't make up a story for a traditional Masai. They are very honest, regal people. Oldtus told me, "Yes, I put a spear through that man."

It was a very picturesque case. The Masai are nomadic herdsmen. In the open field with their cows, they follow nature, the rainfall and so on. Borders, passports, and such modern European innovations mean nothing to them. It would take days to explain to them that one country is administratively different from another. Oldtus and some other young Masai were taking their cattle through a wide area, and this white settler had encircled part of the area as his farm. These Masai didn't know this. Their fathers and grandfathers had been passing through for years. Not only that, but to the Masai, no one "owns" land. Also, they believe that all cattle were originally owned by the Masai and that other people stole the cows they have from them. That is why the Masai are known for stealing cattle. They are taking back as many of their cattle as they can.

Oldtus was not on that man's land to steal his cattle. He was passing through, and probably the farmer's servant shouted to the farmer — "Master, come and look, some Masai are passing cattle through your land." It was not just a matter of trespassing. Whites usually owned thoroughbred cattle, while the Masai had ordinary cattle which might carry East Coast fever, so it was not good for one to mingle with the other.

This white farmer — instead of coming out, waving to them and saying something such as: "Aye man, you want to pass through, all is well, the next waterhole is two miles down" — was an arrogant South African who came out with his automatic rifle and tried to chase them away.

The other Masai ran off with their cows, but Oldtus just stood there. He wasn't used to this. It wasn't that he was being obstinate. He just was not used to being shouted at in a strange language. He stood there with his cows.

The farmer came up to him and tried to grab his spear from him. If you know anything about the Masai, you will never try to take away their spears. His father gave it to him, and he earned it when he came of age and proved himself worthy.

Later, speaking to Oldtus, this is what he told me in his cell while I was preparing for his defence.

"He pulled my spear and I pulled his stick." (The stick in this case being a gun; Oldtus had never seen a gun.)

"Then what did you do?" I asked.

"He pulled my spear and I pulled his stick again."

"And what did you do after that?"

"Then I heard a very loud noise and saw smoke coming from the stick. I felt a pain in my arm."

I looked at Oldtus' arm and saw a long burn mark. The farmer had shot him and grazed his arm.

"Then what did you do?" I said.

Until then, Oldtus had not taken any of this tugging seriously. He though it was some sort of game, pulling at the spear and then the stick. But after the big sound and the smoke he said:

"I realized that he wanted to hurt me, so I pulled away the spear and put it through him."

"What did you do then?"

"He fell down and I pulled the spear out."

"Where did it go?"

He pointed to the middle of his chest and said: "It went through here and came out here"; then he pointed to his back.

Then Oldtus wiped the spear off on the grass and went on with his cows.

The news came out and the police went on a manhunt. They thought it was a Masai who was part of Mau Mau and reported that they were looking for a dangerous man who had killed a European. Driving around for the next few days I saw groups of Masai huddled together outside police stations. They were catching them and bringing them in by the dozens, questioning them, beating them to find out the name of the murderer.

Oldtus eventually heard that the police were looking for him so he walked into the district of Sanya Juu and went to the district commissioner. He said, "I am the man you are looking for." The commissioner turned out to be a very decent man. Actually, he was the brother of Peter Townsend, the man whom it was rumoured Princess Margaret had once wanted to marry. This district commissioner calmly wrote down his confession and a full report of what had happened, and arrested him.

Shortly after this, I was visiting a European farm not far from Moshi. I'd heard that a white rhinoceros had been caught and I wanted to take some pictures. Also I wanted to look around. They kept all sorts of animals on this farm — snakes, zebras, monkeys — which they sometimes sold to zoos. I spent the afternoon there and then, on my way home, I decided to stop at my office and pick up some mail.

Outside my office I saw a group of about fifteen Masai, some elders and some younger men with spears, and in the centre a very short white man. The European, who was a priest, spoke to me in Swahili. They had all walked about eighty miles. The chiefs had learned about me and wanted my help in Oldtus' case. I told them it was a bit late in the day — and it was Saturday — but invited them to come into the office to talk to me. The priest said, "No they won't come inside. They're not used to being inside a house." My office was on the ground floor with a piazza outside shared by the various offices in the building. I told the priest to explain to them that it wasn't a good idea for them to tell me their business outside, where anyone could overhear. He explained, and they reluctantly and suspiciously came in, looking around carefully, quite unused to being indoors. They refused to sit preferring to stand, leaning slightly on their spears.

The priest told me the story of Oldtus, and then said the Masai were not asking me to defend him. They wanted me to take money to the court, and give it to the judge so that Oldtus could be returned to them to be tried by their laws.

I had to explain that since the British had come, there were new laws. I showed them the books behind me and said they were filled with all the laws, and that one of these laws said that if a man kills another when he is not supposed to, he will be hanged. The Masai elder who had been doing all the talking suddenly looked at me strangely, as if to say: "What are you, some kind of young fool?" Then they all began talking among themselves.

I asked the priest what they were saying. He explained. "They want you to pay for him to come out so they can try him, because if what you say is true and they hang him, who will pay the bride-price for the second widow who must return to her empty bed?"

This is the strongest argument I have ever heard against capital punishment.

In their law, if a man kills another man, he has robbed that widow of her husband. He is then sentenced to pay her so many cows and so many goats, according to the importance of the man who has been killed. If the murderer cannot pay, then he has to work as a slave for that widow for the rest of his life, to compensate for the loss of her husband. So these Masai thought that having already killed one man, if the murderer was hanged, there would be two widows left behind to go to their empty beds. What they were saying to me is: "your law is a stupid law, why are you going to have two men killed? Give him back to us so he can pay the bride-price to that other man's widow."

"The law is now very different," I explained. But I told them we would go to court and see what could be done.

"Now?" they asked.

"No, it's Saturday evening."

"Well can we take him home now?"

"No, the judge has to see him first."

The following week I went to visit Oldtus in prison. He was like a bird in a cage. He wouldn't eat their prison food — mashed cornmeal and boiled meat. If you gave Oldtus the most deliciously cooked chicken, caviar or baked fish, he wouldn't touch it. The Masai follow a very strict and limited diet, as I said before. I don't know how they feed Masai in prison. I am sure many of them die there.

We went to court soon afterwards. The police were trying to frame him as a cattle-thief and use that as his motive for murder.

They brought in two eminent doctors. Both had met together and conferred about the evidence they would give. The whole case was drenched in prejudice. The doctors were there to prove that Oldtus had not killed in self-defence. By showing how the organs had been penetrated, that is, in what sequence, they said the victim had to have been lying down when he was killed. The first doctor said all this, and then the second doctor came in and gave the same bogus testimony — only he completely reversed the sequence by which the organs were penetrated by the spear.

I cross-examined both: "Are you quite sure that this was so? That if he were lying down they could not have been penetrated in any other way?"

Both answered, "Yes."

I asked the second doctor if he had examined the prisoner.

This produced a great deal of tittering among the Europeans in court — the idea of this eminent white doctor examining a Masai.

He said, "No."

I said: "Don't you know you should examine both the victim and the prisoner?"

"Sometimes we do, and sometimes we don't."

"Will you examine him now?" I asked. "Do you see a scar on his arm?"

"Obviously an old scar," he said, and for the court's entertainment added, "Probably got it climbing through barbed wire to steal cattle."

Again the court room was filled with laughter. "Doesn't it look like a burn to you?" I asked.

"No," he said confidently, "any fool can see that's not a burn."

I knew that the district commissioner had dutifully examined the prisoner at the time of his arrest and had written down in his report that he noticed the burn mark. I repeated my question to the doctor, and again he pronounced that "any fool" could see that it was not a burn.

Having got that established from his mouth, I then said: "Would it surprise you to hear that the prisoner was examined by the district com- missioner shortly after he was arrested, that by the law the arresting officer must always report the physical condition of a prisoner, that this is written into the Evidence Act?" and I cited the relevant section.

The district commissioner was himself sitting in the court. I pointed to him: "Would you describe this district commissioner as a fool?" I asked. The doctor did not answer. I repeated the question a number of times.

Finally the judge said: "I think you're playing that one a bit too much, Mr. Thompson."

"I want an answer," I said.

"I think you've made the point," said the judge.

Other evidence made it clear that it was not a case of wanton murder as the crown tried to make out. It was a clear act of self-defence on the part of Oldtus-Bin-Lisau. He was acquitted. This was Tanganyika. Perhaps in Kenya it would have been otherwise. During the trial the other Masai had been sitting outside, staring in through the windows, not understanding anything that was going on — simply wanting Oldtus returned to them alive. In the meantime, Oldtus and I had become great friends.

His spear had been in my possession during the trial, as evidence. Now he wanted it back, but I had decided to take it as payment and told him: "No, this is my spear now." He understood, and I brought it back with me to Jamaica, where it remains as a souvenir.

Josephine Muthoni and son, Lawrence. Jamaica, 1971

With Jomo Kenyatta, Kenya, 1973

With His Imperial Majesty Haile Selassie of Ethiopia

Dudley Thompson, ca. 1970s

With Fidel Castro, Cuba, 1977

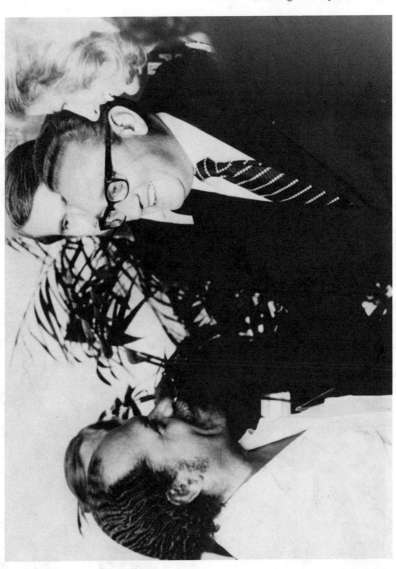

With U.S. Secretary of State, Henry Kissinger

Dudley Thompson and Margaret Cezair Thompson, Elmina Castle, Ghana, 1991

Epilogue

Over the years I returned to East Africa several times to visit my old friends Kenyatta, Nyerere and others. In May 1963, Kenya had its first election based on full franchise, and Kenyatta's party, the KAU, received an overwhelming mandate. Kenyatta became the first president of Kenya and remained so for the rest of his life.

A year earlier in 1962, my own country received its independence, and I remember the strong emotion I felt seeing along with my children the Union Jack brought down, and the Jamaican flag in black, green and gold hoisted up for the first time, in the National Stadium. I felt no less joyful when I attended Kenya's independence ceremony at the Uhuru Stadium in Nairobi in 1963. The stadium was filled with music and dancing. The rhythmic stamping of thousands of feet joyously and untiringly seemed to come from the very depths of the earth of Africa. Many dignitaries were present. The Duke of Edinburgh represented the English crown. Mrs. Indira Gandhi was among the V.I.P.'s present and this was my first meeting with her. She was not yet prime minister of India. I found her a very strong personality, a courteous and exceptionally intelligent woman. Special guests included Edna Clark, Kenyatta's English wife, and their son Peter, who were were warmly welcomed into the family by Kenyatta's African wives and children. D. N. Pritt was there and also Jomo's long-time friend Dinah Stock. Mr. Thurgood Marshall, the highly respected Justice of the supreme court of the USA, was one of the specially invited guests.

The day of my arrival in Kenya for the independence celebrations, is a day I will never forget. As the plane landed in Nairobi with many international dignitaries on board, we were told that we could not disembark for a while. I looked through the window and saw a grey Lincoln Conti-

135

nental drive up to the plane, and out of it came Jomo Kenyatta. Immediately, hundreds of African women who had been standing along the railing let out a terrific and strange sound — "woo-woo-woo-woo-woo," an ululation from the backs of their throats — that seemed to go on forever, and people began to surround Jomo or "Mzee," as he was known. He shook their hands, towering over most of them. Everyone seemed to worship the ground he walked on. I have never seen such a genuine show of affection between a leader and his people.

He sent an aide on board and asked if Mr. Dudley Thompson could disembark first. The red carpet had already been rolled out. "Mzee" and other government ministers stood in line to receive all their guests. I came down the steps of the plane, and there was Jomo, the old man, waiting for me, hugging me with tears in his eyes. He said Ngina, his wife, was at home preparing a special pea soup for me. I was overwhelmed. After so many years he remembered my favourite African dish, and on this important day of Kenya's history, his wife had stayed home to prepare it. He turned to everyone and said: "you remember Bwana Wakili Thompson" — which is what people had called me in East Africa. "Dudley," he said, "I will never forget that cake you brought for me that first Christmas in prison." This was the memory of a true friend.

Tanganyika had also celebrated its independence in 1961, and united with Zanzibar to form Tanzania in 1964. I remember Nyerere sending me a long effusive cable telling me the date of independence was set. With the birth of these two African republics I felt very satisfied with the work that I had taken part in. Both Kenyatta and Nyerere asked me to stay and work in their countries, and I might have been very happy, having had such a romance with Africa, to have lived there and built up a lucrative practice. But it was now time to help "cleanup the mess on my own doorstep," as Norman Manley had reminded me. I remained very close to both Kenyatta and Nyerere and paid several official visits in later years to East Africa, representing the Jamaican government. Also, Nyerere made an official visit to Jamaica, and I was very happy to have him in my own home and to introduce him to the youngest of my children, Margaret and Kathy, who had been born after I left Africa.

In 1978 Kenyatta died and I was invited, both officially and by the family, to attend his funeral. I was received by several ministers and old friends at the Nairobi airport, and after, with many heads of state and a throng of several hundred thousand people, I paid my last respects and laid a wreath at the sarcophagus where for days and nights there was an endless stream of visitors paying last respects to "Mr. Africa." As the crowd filed past they saw their dear "Mzee" for the last time, impeccably dressed with a rose as ever in his button hole and his distinctive gold ring with outsized stone. But perhaps I was the only person who noticed the gold chapareta around his wrist which he had worn for years with this inscription — "To my dear friend Mzee, President of Kenya, from Dudley Thompson, Jamaica."

He was an astute politician, an outstanding statesman in the international field, a nationalist who set Kenya on a peaceful and shady foundation, avoiding problems of racial animosity and arranging for a smooth succession of power when he passed away in August 1978.

Thus ended a great chapter in my life. I remember sitting in the court houses of colonial Kenya, participating in the administration of British justice, and feeling a very lonely man. My only strength, having grown up in colonial Jamaica and studied as a Rhodes Scholar at Oxford, was that I understood the system which was causing the pain. The Africans had faith in me because I seemed unafraid to confront the British on their behalf. But I usually felt quite unworthy of that faith. I had not long since been a colonial school teacher in the simple country backwoods of Jamaica, and as a child I had marched to the town square with the others on Empire Day, holding up my Union Jack. Imperialism, whether it shows itself in the classroom or the courtroom, is a most formidable enemy. Also, the relationship of the colonial to the empire as a whole is a very complicated one. The empire I fought for in World War II I fought against only a few years later at Kapenguria, in the most important political trial I have ever been involved in. Today I know that the only real failure is not trying to destroy that fear — that fear to confront the enemy on all sides and in all its various forms.

Do small countries such as Jamaica play a part in the world events that shape our future? I think they do. If superpowers were the sole repository of wisdom, India could not have produced Mahatma Gandhi. The military might and development of France and the United States separately and successively failed to dominate and conquer the spirit of Ho Chi Minh. It is true that these were exceptional men, but they used tools fashioned out of their traditions and history — and they won. The lesson is clear, that at a time when the world is tottering on the brink of suicide by the activation of weapons of mass destruction, that at this very time we are seeing a redistribution of thought in an interdependent world, including the group described as "non-aligned." More and more nations of the world are seeking the banner of true independence. The Third World is a growing reality, and its people are becoming more vocal in their demand for peace. It is they who are educating the world in the priorities of peace and the struggle for survival.

INDEX

Books from the Majority Press

THE NEW MARCUS GARVEY LIBRARY

Literary Garveyism: Garvey, Black Arts and the Harlem Renaissance. Tony Martin. $19.95 (cloth), $9.95 (paper).

The Poetical Works of Marcus Garvey. Tony Martin, Ed. $17.95 (cloth), $9.95 (paper).

Marcus Garvey, Hero: A First Biography. Tony Martin. $19.95 (cloth), $8.95 (paper).

The Pan-African Connection. Tony Martin. $22.95 (cloth), $10.95 (paper).

Message to the People: the Course of African Philosophy. Marcus Garvey. Ed. by Tony Martin. $22.95 (cloth), $9.95 (paper).

Race First: The Ideological and Organizational Struggles of Marcus Garvey and the Universal Negro Improvement Association. Tony Martin. $29.95 (cloth), $10.95 (paper).

The Philosophy and Opinions of Marcus Garvey. Amy Jacques Garvey, Ed. $12.95 (paper).

Amy Ashwood Garvey: Pan-Africanist, Feminist and Wife No. 1. Tony Martin. Forthcoming.

African Fundamentalism: A Literary and Cultural Anthology of Garvey's Harlem Renaissance. Tony Martin, Ed. $14.95 (paper).

THE BLACK WORLD

Brazil: Mixture or Massacre? Essays in the Genocide of a Black People. Abdias do Nascimento. $12.95 (paper).

Studies in the African Diaspora: A Memorial to James R. Hooker (1929-1976). John P. Henderson and Harry A. Reed, Eds. $39.95 (cloth).

In Nobody's Backyard: The Grenada Revolution in its Own Words. Vol. I, the Revolution at Home. Tony Martin, Ed. $22.95 (cloth). **Vol. II, Facing the World.** Tony Martin, Ed. $22.95 (cloth).

Guinea's Other Suns: The African Dynamic in Trinidad Culture. Maureen Warner-Lewis. $9.95 (paper).

Carlos Cooks: And Black Nationalism from Garvey to Malcolm. Robert, Nyota and Grandassa Harris, Eds. $9.95 (paper).

From Kingston to Kenya: The Making of a Pan-Africanist Lawyer. Dudley Thompson, with Margaret Cezair Thompson. $10.95 (paper).

Order from The Majority Press, P.O. Box 538, Dover, MA 02030, U.S.A. Mass. residents add 5% sales tax.